MEN OF ALAMEIN

THE AUTHOR IN CONSULTATION WITH MAJ. GEN. D.N. WIMBERLEY DSO., MC., COMMANDER OF THE 51ST HIGHLAND DIVISION, DURING THE LATER STAGES OF THE BATTLE OF ALAMEIN.

MEN OF ALAMEIN

BY

Colonel C. P. S. Denholm-Young OBE, P.S.C.

SPA BOOKS
with
TOM DONOVAN PUBLISHING

© Colonel C. P. S. Denholm-Young 1987

All rights reserved. No part of this publication may be reproduced, stored in a retrieval system, or transmitted, in any form by any means, electrical, mechanical or otherwise without first seeking the written permission of the copyright owner and of the publisher.

ISBN: 0–907590–23–3

Publishing history: This work was first issued in Cairo in 1943 and has been out of print for many years. This work has never previously been published in Great Britain and this edition reproduces the original text complete and unabridged with the addition of contemporary photographs.

Published by SPA BOOKS LTD in association with
              TOM DONOVAN PUBLISHING LTD
              PO Box 47
              STEVENAGE
              Herts SG2 8UH

Printed in Great Britain by The Bath Press, Avon

CONTENTS

	PAGE
THE SIGNALS PREPARE	1
INFANTRY SUBALTERN	17
OCTOBER 23RD 1942	24
BATTLE	37
DOGFIGHT	49
DON R	69
SIGNALS AGAIN	80
THROUGH AT LAST	92
INTERLUDE	110
FIVE DAYS' LEAVE	130
CHRISTMAS	151
THE WADI CHEBIR	167
THE BATTLE OF THE WADI ZEM ZEM	179
AMBUSH	193
HOMS — TRIPOLI	211
EPILOGUE	230
ILLUSTRATIONS	between pages 118–119

To my Sister

FOREWORD

This book is not a history, nor is it intended to be a statement of events in the order in which they happened. It is an attempt to recapture something of the spirit of adventure which permeated the whole of that wonderful body of fighting men whom the world knows as the Eighth Army. The author had the honour to fight with that Army all the long way from El Alamein across the sands of the Libyan Desert to Tripoli. Many of the scenes set forth in this book are therefore very much founded upon facts as they happened during those wonderful ninety days. It was a long fight and a weary one, but these sketches adapted from the lives of some of those who took part in this great adventure will help to show how great was the spirit of comradship and the will to win amongst the men of the Desert Army. Even when the fighting was hard and conditions were at their worst, even when there was little water and less alcohol, there was always friendship and a merry laugh to cheer us on our way in those days when we hunted and harried the Invader across the Desert Sands.

C.P.S.D-Y.

Extract from a letter to the author from Major-General D. N. Wimberley CB, DSO, MC, commander of 51st Highland Division in North Africa and Sicily, written in 1943:

'My dear Denholm,
    Thank you very much for the copy of your book which I shall value very much. I never stopped reading your book after I had taken it up until I finished it. I fear it interfered for a few hours with other duties! I enjoyed it a lot and it brought back so many memories that it will be a pleasant companion to have all one's life. It is much more than that though, it will, I feel, bring home more than ever to the people of Scotland what they owe to our Jocks. So you deserve not mere thanks from me, but thanks from all Highland Division men for what you have done in putting your story of life in the H.D. across in an interesting and amusing way, and giving such a true picture of life in Divisional Signals, and a balanced picture of war as a whole.
                      Yours aye,
                            Douglas Wimberley.'

CHAPTER I

THE SIGNALS PREPARE

IT WAS HOT IN THE DUG-OUT, ALMOST UNBEARABLY hot, and the place was over-crowded into the bargain. In addition to the Colonel and the Adjutant, there were three clerks and two cipher N.C.O.'s. Every occupant of the small room was immersed in his own particular job. There were two telephones on the small table which the Colonel was sharing with the Adjutant, and in one of the corners stood an intricate looking wireless set. A twisted rope of field telephone cables was strung from the roof. It was the office of the Commanding Officer of a Divisional Signals.

One of the telephones rang and the Adjutant answered it.

"Morgan here," he said. "Who's that ? ADMS*? Just a minute, Sir, I'll ask the C.O. to speak." Turning, he handed the instrument to him. "Colonel Galsworthy to speak to you, Sir."

"Right," said the Colonel, grasping the telephone, "That you, Doc ? Are you coming round with me ? ...Good. I'll be free in about five minutes, will that do ? ...It will. Grand. I'll meet you at my Jeep in five minutes time. Good-bye."

---

* The Senior Medical Officer. – Assistant Director of Medical Services

"I'm off round the Brigades and Regiments with the ADMS," he said to the Adjutant. "There's precious little more I can do here now. Tell Major Carter that he has just got to see that the Northern buried route is in working order by the end of the day. I'm counting on that as a spare if the Southern bury goes west. And you might give James Greig a ring to see if that hundred miles of twisted cable has fetched up at his dump yet. My few remaining hairs will go grey if it doesn't get there by noon to-day. One more thing, if Alec rings up, tell him we'll look in at Tac H.Q.* later in the afternoon, just to see if everything is well. Expect me back by six in the evening; and don't drink all the remaining whisky, you thirsty devil!"

"Not much fear of that, Sir," grinned the Adjutant. "There's salt in the water again."

The Colonel left the dug-out and made his way along the dark passage-way up towards the daylight. His office was only one of many which had been constructed in the hill-side on the stretch of land between the coast road and the sea, on the Eastern fringe of the desert near Alamein Station. He paused at the entrance, to let his eyes become accustomed to the glare of the sun. Away to the North lay the sea, shimmering in the tropical heat of an autumn day in Egypt. To the West was the ridge of desert and rocks where the army was massing for the great onslaught of the next day. Up the road came an incessant stream of lorries, bringing supplies and ammunition

---

* The Advanced Battle Headquarters.

for the hundreds of guns which had been cunningly concealed during the last week. A few of these were letting off at intervals, just as they had been doing for the last few weeks, ever since Rommel had been halted here in his desperate drive towards the Delta.

The Colonel lit a cigarette and walked over to the car-park, where his driver was waiting with the ever faithful Jeep.

" 'Morning, Wilson." The driver saluted him smartly. "Have you seen anything of Colonel Galsworthy? He's coming round with us to-day."

"That's him coming now, Sir," said Wilson, nodding towards a figure walking from the direction of 'A'* Mess.

"The top of the morning to you, Doctor dear, I trust I see you well," grinned the Colonel to the approaching officer.

" 'Morning, Master Twiddler," the ADMS answered. "Any news of import this morning?"

"What a name to call a chap at this time of the morning," laughed the Colonel.

"It's your own fault for being such a wizard with the Mess wireless set."

The Doctor was a tall, weather-beaten man of about fifty years. He looked what he was, as fit as a fiddle, and he wore the medal ribbons of the last war on his chest, and the D.S.O. into the bargain. He had been in the Division longer than any other officer, and many were the officers and men who owed much to his kindness and cheery smile, unfailing

---

* The G.O.C's Mess.

even when things were at their worst, and the shells were dropping round about.

They got into the little Jeep, the driver sat at the back and the Colonel drove himself. They moved out on to the coast road and headed Eastwards, back down the line in the direction of Alexandria. A mile or so and they passed the military policeman standing at the junction of Springbok Road. Carrying straight on, they made their first stop at Alam el Milkh. Here was the Headquarters of the Administrative services of their Division. They left the driver to take the Jeep away from the entrance, and made their way down into the dug-outs, which were alive with men hurrying hither and thither, making the last arrangements for the big attack.

There are many people who think of armies as being made up of infantrymen who carry rifles and stick bayonets into the enemy, and of artillerymen who fire the guns. But they never consider the thousands of others who are every bit as important, but who never come into the limelight. There are the men who ferry up the supplies and the ammunition for the guns ; there are those who man the workshops without which no vehicle could remain for long in service ; there are the medical orderlies and surgeons who attend to the wounded and the sick ; and there are those men of the Signal Service who lay and maintain thousands of miles of field telephone cables, often under heavy fire from the guns of the enemy, without any hope of hitting back, and who manage to operate and repair intricate wireless sets which pass vital messages back to headquarters when those who are directing the battles require accurate information as to how things are going.

Colonel Peter Denman was the last man who would detract one little bit from the dangers and hardships of the front-line soldier, but it had often occurred to him as one of the Signal Service, that whereas between periods of action the infantry and artillery could sit down and snatch a spell of well-earned rest and sleep, his men had to carry on their all-important task of maintaining vital communications, come what might. They could never afford to relax for one single moment. Battle or no battle, day or night, his men had to carry on, working by reliefs, so that news and orders might be transmitted at any hour of the day or night. His was an interesting job, but it never ended. He was on perpetual duty. If one of his many wireless sets went wrong, he had to know all about it ; if one of his hundreds of miles of telephone cable went out of order, it worried him until it had been put right.

They made their way down into the Signal Office. Here was a bustle of activity. Orderlies were coming and going with their messages for the Administrative Staff. At one end of the dug-out stood the telephone exchange, where two operators sat with the headphones strapped to their heads. The exchange was busy, and the indicators were dropping left and right. Down one side of the small room were seated four operators, working morse instruments to Signal Offices down the line. The Signalmaster hovered round the place like a hen watching her chicks.

The Colonel walked up to the Signalmaster, a serious looking young Captain who had been in the Civil Service in London in private life.

"All well, Joe?" he asked, with a smile.

"Not too bad, Sir," was the reply. "We've had a spot of bother with the line to Rear Corps, but I've had two men out on it for the last hour. I hope it will be through any time now."

"Don't worry, that's all you can do. They'll find the fault soon enough. How are you off for Despatch Riders?"

"I've only got three, Sir. Do you think you could possibly get us a Jeep, or perhaps two?" The young Captain looked expectant. "These motor bikes are no bloody good at all in the desert, Sir."

"You're telling me. I've told the General many times, and he is very sympathetic, but he says that he can't make the things out of sand. They just don't exist."

The Colonel passed round the dug-out, having a word of greeting for every man there. He seemed to know them all and where they came from, back home. The exchange operators both came from Edinburgh and had been in the North British Insurance Company when the war broke out. The Sergeant superintendant was a policeman from Inverness, and two of the orderlies hailed from Clydeside. Peter Denman himself came from Dumfries, where his family had lived in the same house for over four hundred years. They were all Scots together, bound with that love of country which is inherant in those from across the Border, and each one of them was determined to see Rommel and all his hordes driven from the soil of Egypt and back along the desert roadway whence they came.

The ADMS came back into the Signal Office. "Are you ready to go on, Twiddler ?" he asked.

"All right, I just want one last word with the chaps here. Listen, you fellows," he said to the men in the room. "To-morrow is the day we have all been waiting for. The big attack is due to start to-morrow night at ten o'clock. As you know, we have been preparing for it for the last six weeks. All those exercises we have been doing were just rehearsals for the real thing. I couldn't tell you at the time, as you probably realise, but the day has come at last. We are going to get our revenge for St. Valerie, and we are going to knock the Bosche for six, right out of North Africa. We have a great superiority in men, tanks and guns, so we shall be on the winning side, for a change. There is not one shadow of doubt about the result — provided each one of us does his job. The Jocks up in the line are going to have a tough time. We don't have to stick a bayonet in the Germans or the Ities. We don't have to march into machine-gun fire. But ours is a job of great responsibility, for it is up to us to see that all orders and messages get to their destinations with the least possible delay. We shall be bombed and we shall be shelled : we shall be well and truly in the battle. But it is up to every one of us to see that we do our job to the very best of our ability, and to ensure that not by any laxity on our part shall the show be let down.

"I'll read you the Army Commander's Order of the Day. It is a personal message to each one of you. He says,

> When I assumed command of the Eighth Army I said that the mandate was to destroy Rommel and his Army and that it would be done as soon as we were ready.
>
> We are ready *now*.
>
> The battle which is now about to begin will be one of the decisive battles of history. It will be the turning point of the war. The eyes of the whole world will be on us, watching anxiously which way the battle will swing.
>
> We can give them their answer at once: "It will swing our way".
>
> We have first-class equipment; good tanks; good anti-tank guns; plenty of artillery and plenty of ammunition; and we are backed up by the finest air striking force in the world.
>
> All that is necessary is that each one of us, every officer and man, should enter this battle with the determination to see it through — to fight and to kill — and finally, to win.
>
> If we do all this, there can be only one result— together we will hit the enemy for 'six', right out of North Africa.
>
> The sooner we win this battle, which will be the turning point of the war, the sooner we shall all get back home to our families.
>
> Therefore, let every officer and man enter the battle with a stout heart, and with the determina-

tion to do his duty so long as he has breath in his body.

And let no man surrender so long as he is unwounded and can fight.

Let us all pray that 'the Lord mighty in battle' will give us the victory.

M. E. F.
23-10-42

B. L. MONTGOMERY.
Lieutenant-General G.O.C.-in-C. Eighth Army
Middle East Forces

"I have one more message for you." It also is a personal message for each one of you, and is from our own Divisional Commander. He says,

"As being in the proud position of Commander of The Highland Division of Scotland, I know that that I am expressing for us all what every Scotsman feels in his heart to-day:

'Scotland for ever, and Second to None!' "

 *   *
 *

The Colonel and the ADMS clambered once more into the little Jeep and drove away in the direction of the Bombay Road. All the way along the coast road was a constant stream of lorries, tanks and guns, making their way up to the front at El Alamein. There were lorries full of South Africans, lorries full of Indians, Staff cars carrying brass hatted Exalted Ones, big ugly anti-aircraft guns, manned by men from all corners of the British Isles. Australians soldiers, wearing their own distinctive headgear, were at work on the telegraph route running on the seaward side of the road. It was a truly Empire Army which was gathering its strength to attack Rommel and his hordes on the morrow.

The traffic was nothing like what it had been earlier in the week, for all the really important units and convoys had long since passed up the route towards the front to their appointed places, and the infantry would not move up till after dark that night. The battalions were resting farther back near El Amayid, preparatory to their night's march, and it was to visit them that the Colonel and the ADMS had come out.

After about seven miles, they came to a military policeman, standing beside a blue triangular pennant denoting the Headquarters of an Infantry Brigade. There was the famous 'HD' sign of the Highland Division and the number of the Brigade in question painted on a wooden board. The Jeep turned off the main road, down into the space set aside for visiting cars.

Getting out, they arranged to meet again in an hour's time and the Colonel made his way to the hole in the ground which denoted the Brigade Major's office. Here he chatted a few moments with the Brigadier and the Brigade Major, making enquiries to ensure that all their Signal requirements were completely satisfied right up to the last minute. Then he left the office and went over to see his own small party of Signallers.

" 'Morning, Bobby," he remarked to a youngish looking Captain who appeared from inside a wireless truck. "How's things?"

"Not too bad, Sir," was the reply. "I've had a hell of a job to recover my cable from the last place we stopped at, but I hear that the last bit has been reeled up within the last half hour."

"Well done you. What about your transport?"

"O.K., Sir. But I don't suppose you can do anything about getting me a Jeep, could you?"

The Colonel laughed; so did the young Captain.

"It's like that, Sir, is it?"

"Not a hope, Bobby. I've tried everything I know to get you some, and it's no good your looking at mine like that, you just can't have it."

"There's no harm in asking, Sir, is there?" grinned Bobby.

"Good Lord, no, but that's as far as you'll get, I'm afraid." They went on talking for a few minutes on technical details of wireless sets and such-like things. Then the Colonel gave Bobby and his men the personal messages from the Army and Divisional Commanders, exactly as he had done earlier on at Rear Divisional Headquarters. Just as he was leaving, Bobby remarked to him : "Have you seen Walter, Sir? I know he wants to see you." Walter, a young relative of Peter, was Signal Officer to a battalion of the Inverness Regiment in Bobby's brigade.

"No, Bobby. I haven't seen him for a week or so. Where is he now?"

"He's only a mile away, Sir, down near the Bombay Road junction."

"All right. I'll go across and see him now." So saying, the Colonel went back to his Jeep and set off to find the Inverness Regiment.

He found it easily, for the Regiment was resting quite near to the main coast road, and only about one mile away. He asked several Jocks the whereabouts of young Walter Mitchell, and finally ran him to earth, sitting amongst a heap of his signal stores.

"Hullo, young fellow. How's life treating you?" he asked with a smile.

"Oh, hullo. Where have you sprung from?" The youngster got to his feet as the older officer stood beside him. He was a remarkably good-looking young man, dressed in a battle-dress blouse and a kilt which had seen some hard service. His face wasn't yet lined with the cares of warfare, and he still had that clean and ruddy complexion of Scotland's youth. The Colonel looked him over affectionately, and felt a pang of sorrow in his heart that this smiling young relative of his had to go forward into the cauldron of an infantry attack on the evening of the next day. What a rotten world it was that demanded that her young men should go off into battle and get killed or maimed for life! Surely Man could find something better to do than to blow his brother man into little pieces? But still, perhaps it was as well, for life would be intolerable under the conditions which Hitler and his gang would impose if the United Nations should lose this conflict.

"How are things, Walter?" he asked at length.

"Not too bad, Peter," smiled the boy. "I'm just having a last look round my stores to see that everything is O.K. for to-morrow."

"Have a cigarette?"

"Thanks very much."

They smoked a while in silence, and then the boy looked up in a slightly embarrased manner.

"I wonder, Peter, if you'd mind looking after these for me?" He produced an envelope from his blouse pocket.

"What is it, Walter?"

"Just a receipt for my things stored with Cooks in Alexandria, and a letter from my Bank in Cairo. If anything happens to me you might look after them for me. Everything I have is to go to my brother John. Will you do this for me, Peter?"

For a moment the Colonel didn't speak. It was a rotten idea, that Walter might get knocked out; but it had to be faced after all.

"Of course I will, Walter," he said with a grin. "But you'll come out of this all right, never fear. We'll have a party at the Crook Inn before very long, I'm sure."

"Thanks awfully, Peter, old chap."

They stood there talking of home and their relatives and friends for a little while. Then Peter had to go off to meet the ADMS. They shook hands and wished each other good luck, promising to compare notes as soon after the battle as they could manage to meet.

The Colonel drove back to the Headquarters of the Brigade where he picked up the ADMS once more. They called at several other units and then turned back towards Alamein and the battle front. It was an easier drive now, for the traffic had thinned out to almost nothing on the road, and they managed to make very good time.

At one battalion, they came on a hardy-looking Jock, sitting on a pile of sandbags, sharpening his bayonet.

"Well, Jock. How do you feel about the battle?" asked the ADMS with a smile. Every Highland soldier answers to the friendly title of 'Jock'.

The man looked up with a broad grin. "Sorr," he said. "When I get in amongst yon," and he nodded his head towards the German lines far away to the West, "I'll give 'em *that* for Paisla', and *that* for Clydebank, and *that* for ma faither in the last War." With each *'that'* he made a vicious thrust with his bayonet.

"Give them just one more for me, Jock," the Colonel laughed, as the two officers passed on their way round the lines of resting troops.

Late in the afternoon, they made their way to the Battle Headquarters from which the General would fight the opening stages of the attack. There were three large holes in the ground, each cunningly camouflaged from observation from the air. One of these was to accomodate the Commander and a few of his staff, one was to be the Signal Centre, and the third was to be a rest place for signal personnel when, if ever, they did manage to snatch a few hours for sleep.

They looked into each in turn, as the Colonel wanted to see that all the many arrangements for telephones and wireless sets had been duly completed; at the Signal Centre he met the officer in charge of the place, one Captain Alec Foster. In private life Foster was a builder in a big way in Kircaldy. He was a cheery soul, and never seemed to be depressed ; a most valuable asset in times of stress.

"Hullo, Alec! Everything all right?"

"Very nearly ready, Sir. I've just got three local lines to lay to-night and the whole thing's finished. But there's one bit of bad news."

"What's that?"

"The Northern bury is pretty well useless, Sir. A cable plough belonging to some other Division has cut right through the bury and burst a water pipe into the bargain. I've got John out with his chaps, doing their best to patch the route up, but I doubt if it will be much use now, owing to induction from the damp."

"Blast all ploughs! Still, do your best, Alec. You can do no more. But I did want to have as many alternatives as I could possibly have. I'll have a word with John on my way back to Division. Any other worries?"

"No, none at all, except a frightful thirst. You couldn't manage to send us up a few cans of beer, could you, Sir?"

"I'll do my best, Alec," the Colonel said with a broad smile. "You'll be starting a sand pit here, I suppose?"

"And spend my holidays here after the War, I don't think."

They passed into the Signal Centre dug-out and inspected the work that had been done. There was an intricate system of telephone exchanges, where several men, stripped to the waist, were hard at their task. Cables were neatly labelled and secured to test frames, and the whole place looked thoroughly businesslike.

The C.O. had a good look round and then prepared to take his departure, along with Colonel Galsworthy, who had just come up, after making a tour of inspection of his Advance Dressing Station in the nearby wadi.

"Cheerio, Alec," said Peter as he got back into his Jeep. "I'll be seeing you at times during the battle."

"Always welcome, Sir," smiled Alec. "But more so with beer."

"I'll do my best." They drove away, in the direction of Divisional Headquarters. On arriving back, the Colonel hurried down to his office, where he found the Adjutant chatting with the old Quartermaster over a mug of tea.

"Anything doing, Tom?" he asked, as he sat down at his rickety table.

"Nothing at all, Sir," replied the Adjutant. "But there are three private letters from Edinburgh for you here."

"Well done, good and faithful one. Let there be peace now, while I read them. Did that cable come to James Greig's dump? I forgot to ask him this morning."

"Arrived this afternoon, Sir."

Peter Denman heaved a sigh of relief. The books were opened and the judgment set. He had done everything that a man could do to ensure that communications within the Division would be first class. It was now up to the individual man to prove his worth, and he had no doubt that his men would do that, each and every one of them. The result was on the lap of the Gods.

He turned contentedly to his letters.

CHAPTER II

INFANTRY SUBALTERN

JOHN GRAY LAY ON HIS BACK AND LOOKED AT the blue sky above him, which was shimmering in the heat of the Egyptian autumn afternoon. All around him lay the men of his battalion, resting after their busy morning, which had been spent in cleaning and oiling their many weapons, and in putting the final touches to their equipment, in readiness for the move forward which they were going to do as soon as it was dark. It was getting on for five in the afternoon, and in a little while the cooks would be ready to serve the evening meal. Meanwhile, both officers and men were taking the chance of a decent rest, well knowing that this might be their last for many days to come.

John Gray was lying a little apart from the rest of his platoon, his broad shoulders pillowed against a small mound of sand. He wore the conventional shirt and shorts of the British soldier, and his webbing equipment was lying at his side. On his shoulders were stitched the Regimental Tarcan of his battalion, together with the famous 'HD' sign of the 51st Highland Division. Only by the two stars on his shoulder-straps could you tell that he was a subaltern. He was, in fact, the officer commanding the platoon which was scattered in the sand hills a short distance away from where he lay.

John was not what you would call an imaginative sort of fellow, and his mind was not filled with any particular apprehension regarding the impending battle. He had never been in battle before, and at his youthful age of twenty-two, the whole proceedings were more or less in the light of a tremendous adventure. He and his platoon had been through some pretty gruelling training exercises during the last five weeks of intensive preparation, so there was no question of himself or any of his men not knowing what to do when the big moment came. His Colonel had seen to that. For many nights the battalion had practiced over and over again just exactly what they were to do on the night of the big attack, when the Eighth Army was to advance over the sands at El Alamein and come to grips with the enemy, who had been waiting there for something like this to happen. Furthermore, John's battalion had already done a week in the particular part of the line where they were to make their attack the following night. He and some of his men had carried out two patrols into No Man's Land, so there would be nothing unfamiliar with the whole proceedings.

The past came surging into John's mind, as he lay there in the sand-hills of Amayid. He found himself thinking of his school days at Watson's College in far off Edinburgh, and he remembered how he felt the day before he was to play in the First Fifteen at Myreside for the first time. There had been a queer little feeling at the pit of his stomach on that day, and he wasn't quite sure now, but there was just a little bit of that same feeling again. But he remembered with a smile, that as soon as he got kicked in the face early in the match in question, he had lost all that nasty feeling in his stomach, and had enjoyed the game just as much as any other game of rugger he had ever played in.

Thoughts came crowding into his brain. He remembered the days at the OCTU* at Dunbar when he had thought the training very hard, and went to his bed every night feeling dog tired. Then he had got used to it and taken these things in his stride. He had left the OCTU and gone off to join the Regiment in the North of Scotland. Everything had seemed very new and strange, but soon he had made friends and now the Regiment seemed to him for all the world like his own home. There were so many good chaps about him, and he was so very keen on his platoon.

He remembered the great day when the Regiment had been visited by the King and Queen. He had felt so proud that day, for the King had stood and spoken to him about his men for quite two minutes. John had never lived through such a wonderful two minutes in his young life.

The voyage out to Africa had been great fun. He had never left Scotland before, and the whole thing had been a tremendous adventure for young John Gray. He had enjoyed calling at the various ports, and getting ashore with a few of his brother subalterns.

There had been the excitement of landing in Egypt, and of getting leave to visit Cairo and all the places he had read about in story books. The Regiment hadn't

---
* Officer Cadet Training Unit

stayed near the flesh pots very long, however, for
they had soon enough started out on the long road to
the Western Desert, where they commenced to train
intensively for the very battle they were to take part
in on the following night.

A shadow fell on his face.

"Come along and have some tea, you lazy blighter."

John looked up and saw the grinning face of Hamish
Macdonald, the commander of another platoon in his
company. He heaved himself to his feet. "That's a
good idea," he said. "I could do with something to
fill the aching void. Come along." They made their
way across to where their batmen were bending over
a petrol fire.

* *
*

It was getting dark, and the men were putting on
their equipment, to the accompaniment of much
swearing and maledictions against Hitler in general
and Rommel in particular, who was responsible for
their having to do that night a fifteen mile march up
towards Alamein. They were to move forward that
night, to occupy small slit trenches, already dug by the
battalions which were now holding the front line.
By lying up in these trenches all the next day until it was
again dark, it was hoped the Germans would not guess
that an enormous number of fresh troops had been
moved up into the line for the big attack. Each man
carried half a sheet of corrugated iron, and protested
to all his gods that these were a damned nuisance ;
but each and all were to bless the mind which thought

of this idea when, later on, they had to cower in their slit trenches, while pieces of shrapnel and machine-gun bullets went whining through the air above them. These little pieces of sheet iron were to save many a man from a nasty wound.

A whistle went and the battalion fell in, ready to move. The roll was called and there was no need to issue any last-minute orders, for they were a well trained battalion, these Invernesshire Regiment lads.

Their Colonel had issued his instructions clearly and without omitting any details which would mean alterations at the last minute.

"Quick march!"

Silently, save for the clinking of weapons, the Regiment moved out, on to the coast road.

Young John Gray was deeply impressed with the beauty of the night. Away to his right lay the sea, almost white in the brilliant moonlight. There was little or no wind, and the great Mediterranean rollers were breaking on the sands with a line of white foam. Occasionally an aeroplane would pass overhead. There was little to be heard, save the rythmic tread of the mens' feet on the roadway. Even this was muffled, as each file of men walked on the sand at the side of the road, leaving the carriageway for the odd vehicles which were still passing up and down. As they got nearer to the front, John could hear occasional field guns firing intermittently, and their flashes made a weird picture against the dark tropical sky.

The Regiment halted regularly every hour, and at about one in the morning they drew level with the observation tower on the opposite side of the road to Alamein Railway Station. A little way further on they turned off, a mile or so down what was known as the Quattara Track, turned again, and John found himself and his platoon marching right in the middle of the gun positions. He couldn't see very much, even in that moonlight, for the mens' feet were raising a great cloud of dust; but every now and again a deafening 'crack' from very near them denoted where a field Battery were letting off their shells in the direction of the enemy's front line.

Suddenly there was a halt, and all officers were called up to the front to meet the Company Commander, one Major Wilson. He was a Regular soldier, and John admired him greatly. Quietly, and without any fuss, the Major issued his orders as to where each platoon was to go.

"John," he said to young Gray, "take your chaps over to near that bit of rising ground, beyond those guns. You will find your slit trenches all dug ready for you. Get your braves into them and make them get down to it and sleep right away. There will be breakfast at half past four, to allow you to be back in your trenches again before it is light. Off you go now, for you'll need all the sleep you can get."

John made his way back to his platoon and got the men on the move. Silently, the little snake of thirty soldiers left the track and wound its way through the gun positions, towards the small dim hulk of rising ground.

"Halt!"

The men stopped in their tracks, while John and his sergeant went on a little way ahead, to have a closer look at the slit trenches. Sure enough, there they were, about twenty small slits in the ground, each capable of taking two men lying down.

"All right, Sergeant Jackson," said John. "Get the Section Sergeants along and tell them where to go. I want No. 2 Platoon over in that corner, the others can sort themselves out here. I shall take this trench here, near the track, and you had better doss down in the one beside me. I want my runner in the next one as well. All right. Get on with it, and don't forget to detail the air sentries for duty, as soon as it gets light."

"Right you are, Sir." The sergeant slipped away into the darkness, to carry out his officer's orders. Ten minutes later the whole platoon was sound asleep in their rat-holes. John Gray walked round his little command, to see that all was well with them, made his way across to where his Company Commander was to be found, reported all correct, came back and lay down in his slit-trench. Guns were still firing at uneven intervals, but John was far too tired to be kept awake by the noise. Let the morrow take care of itself, he was going to sleep.

CHAPTER III

OCTOBER 23rd 1942

COLONEL FORSYTH, THE COMMANDING OFFICER of the Inverness Regiment, awoke with a start to find his batman bending over his slit trench and shaking his shoulder.

"What is it, Tweedie?" he asked peevishly, for he had been very sound asleep, and had only lain down a couple of hours before.

"It's gone four o'clock, Sir, and I've managed to get you a mug of tea." So saying, he knelt down and handed the steaming mug to his master.

"Tweedie, you're a wonder. When I wake up in hell, I expect I shall see you there, waiting for me with a drink of iced water; except that you're far too good a chap to gravitate to the nether regions."

"Well, Sir," grinned the batman, "you know, what you are always telling me?"

"What's that?"

"What's the use of being king if you can't have jam for tea?"

Colonel Forsyth laughed. "I suppose you're right." He took a long drink of tea and then went on. "Run across to Major Wilson and ask him to come over and see me as soon as he can."

"Right you are, Sir," said Tweedie and was gone into the darkness.

The Colonel looked about him. It was still very dark, the moon had set long ago and it was not yet dawn. The guns were firing occasionally, but as far as he could judge, there was no answering fire from the other side of the line. It was quite cool, the night had taken away all the heat of the previous day, and the sun had not yet come up to make the world the hot, fly-ridden place which all soldiers of the Eighth Army will always remember.

"Good-morning, Colonel." The tall figure of Major Wilson appeared beside his slit-trench.

"Hullo, Wilson!" said the Colonel, getting slowly to his feet and climbing out of the trench. "Had a decent sleep?"

"Not too bad, Sir. And you?"

"Only so-so for the first hour. These blasted gunners would let fly just as I was dozing off. But I managed to get to sleep after a bit. Now about the day; I want you to see that all your braves have their breakfast and get back into their trenches again before it is light. And there must be no question of any man getting out again during the hours of daylight. The battle has started now for the Infantry, and it would ruin everything if we went and gave the show away at this stage of the proceedings."

"I'll see to it, Sir", said Wilson. "I have already given most precise orders on the same subject. I take it there is no harm if I come over and see you during the day, is there, Sir?"

"None at all, Wilson. In fact, I mean to have a Company Commanders' conference during the afternoon. But we'll have that away from the battalion, as I don't want the men to see the officers walking about, when they have to remain put in their beastly holes."

"What time will you want us, Sir?"

"Make it three o'clock. I'll tell the noble Adjutant to let you all know. I'd do it this morning, but I think that the Brigade Commander will be here with the General during the morning, if I am not mistaken."

"I can't see the General staying away from us to-day, Sir."

"Nor can I. I should think, that when the battle starts, the G1* will have the very devil of a job in restraining him from personally leading the foremost platoon."

Both officers laughed.

"I'll away to see my chaps' breakfasts, Sir."

"All right, old boy. I'm going to have a spot to eat myself. See you in a wee whilie."

Major Wilson saluted and went off to rejoin his company, where the men were getting out of their little slits in the ground and congregating in small groups.

As it started to get light, the officers and N.C.O's bustled round, getting the men back underground, and in a very short time there was precious little left to show that nearly a thousand men were hidden within a very small area. Colonel Forsyth walked round his unit to see that his orders had been carried

---

* The Senior General Staff Officer.

out. He paused here and there to have a word with an officer or a man. Everywhere he went, he was greeted with a smile and a cheery word, for he was of the very best type of Commanding Officer. He knew almost every man in his battalion, and their little worries were his worries. He was plentifully endowed with the Human Touch, and had that great art of putting men at their ease when he talked with them, and yet, he never lost any of his authority by so doing.

An officer ought to take a personal pride in his particular body of men. They are *his* little part of the show, and it is up to him to see that they get every chance of proving that they are the best platoon, or the best company of the best battalion of the best Army in the world. He must know them intimately. He must know where they come from and what they were doing before they were called up, or joined the Army.

Colonel Forsyth passed along amongst his men as a trusted friend and leader. They all knew that if he had anything to do with it, they would be put into the battle with every possible chance of success.

After completing his rounds, he returned to his own trench and lay down to get a couple of hours' sleep before the General and the Brigadier arrived.

* * *

The sun was not long in getting up above the horizon. It was the 23rd of October 1942, and the days were still uncomfortably hot in Northern Egypt. The

Headquarters of the Highland Division were very lucky as they were established on the high ground overlooking the sea, not far from Alamein Station itself. The place was just off the main road, and commanded a grand panorama of the battle front. Away to the West, one could see the ridge which marked the last outpost of that part of the Eighth Army's front, for beyond this ridge was the foremost minefield through which our troops would pass that night, after dark. It was here, and here only, that the United Nations were going to take the offensive. True, other attacks were about to be made on other, widely varying fronts. But it was at El Alamein that the turning point of the War was going to be reached, and from then on the Allies were going to call the tune, and to no mean extent.

Looking Westwards in that early morning, officers of the Divisional Staff could see a multitude of little fires springing up from the desert, where men were cooking their breakfast in petrol tins. As far as the eye could see, and it could see about five miles, there were small black dots signifying groups of men and vehicles or gun positions. To the South, making three straight lines running East and West, were the tracks known as 'Sun', 'Moon' and 'Star'. These had been cleared with infinite care, and were marked every hundred yards or so with a metal Sun, Moon or Star at the top of a pole. Along these tracks would come the hundreds of tanks which were to be loosed through the gaps which the infantry divisions had the task of opening in the enemy's lines. Never before in the history of war had such an enormous armoured force been conceived, and the mind boggled at what would be the result of letting loose this force of battleships of the land behind the German lines. If only one could be certain that there would be no hitch. If only one could be sure that the Sappers would be able to clear sufficient gaps in the enemy minefields, through which our tanks could be slipped. If only...! But there lies the eternal apprehension of the battlefield. No commander can ever foretell exactly what is going to happen. No man of that Eighth Army doubted that the armoured forces would eventually get through behind the enemy, but how long it would take — that was a very different matter.

Peter Denman, the Signals Colonel had done all that he could do to ensure that the communications of his Division would be first-class. He had visited personally all the little sections of his widely scattered unit, to make sure that they lacked nothing in the way of personnel or equipment. He had seen every single infantry battalion and all of the artillery, and everything which came within his jurisdiction was as nearly perfect as he could make it. Now there was nothing else to be done but wait as patiently as possible for the battle to start, and that was not till ten o'clock that night. So, in the meantime, he decided to pay a visit to Corps Headquarters, where he would find his technical superior, the Chief Signal Officer, and discuss with him the laying on of stocks of equipment and men to meet the inevitable battle casualties which were bound to happen.

The Colonel got into his waiting Jeep and drove off, down the coast road in the direction of Alamein. When they got to Springbok Road, they turned off, towards the sea. Down across the sandy waste, they threaded their way until they came to a pretty decent track, leading across the salt marshes. There was a broad causeway, capable of taking two largish cars at a time, and the little Jeep quickly crossed this death trap; for it was no place to be caught in a car by a lurking enemy fighter plane. All that one could do, would be to drive on, in the hope that the pilot would either not attempt to attack, or miss the moving car.

At the far side of this causeway, they turned off and struck the sand dunes beside the sea. They wound about for a few hundred yards and eventually came upon the C.S.O's office vehicle, cunningly concealed in a little hollow.

The Colonel got out and climbed into the bigger lorry.

"Morning, Sir," he said as he passed through the doorway.

The older man looked up from his desk. "Hullo, Peter. Come along in and sit you down."

"Thanks," said the Colonel, and slipped along the narrow office to a revolving chair beside the Chief Signal Officer. It was a neat little office, holding the Chief, two Staff Officers and a wireless operator. Down each side were fitted shelves, which accomodated a multitude of files and documents. At the top end, at a table set across the car, sat the Chief Signal Officer, Colonel Marston.

"How's things this morning, Peter?" he asked with a smile. "Are all your marvellous lines working yet?"

"Not too bad, Sir. I've had a spot of bother with the Norther Bury. Some fool went and ran a cable plough through it yesterday morning, but I've managed to lay another seven pairs through that gap. But I wish to goodness these blokes would ask me before they come steaming around my preserves with their blasted ploughs. Could you get an order issued to cover this, do you think, Sir?"

"Yes, Peter, I certainly will. It was very naughty of them to do that without asking me beforehand. Now about stores; have you got all you want for just now?"

"Quite all right for the moment, Sir, but I'll be certain to be at you for telephones and cable later on. I propose that James Greig gives your stooge a ring every evening. How will that do?"

"Splendid. But do try to let me have as much notice as possible. My cupboard isn't all that full, you know."

"I'll do all I can, Sir," replied Peter with a smile. "By the way, I'm all right for men at the moment, but I still need a subaltern for the Lame Man's Brigade. Young Douglas is still in hospital with jaundice, and it will be another three weeks before he comes out. Can you hold out any hope of getting a replacement before long? It is very hard on the wretched Spike to have to carry on on his own all this time."

"Well, Peter. You know what it is. You cagy Scotsmen won't take anyone who doesn't hail from

North of the Tweed. I suppose you can't expect a mere Englishman to speak your mystic language. But if you do want to get your own chaps back, you've just got to wait for them. If I get you a replacement for Douglas now, it means that it might not be a Scot, and there you would be saddled with him, and Douglas would have to be sent to some other unit when he comes out of hospital. It's all a vicious circle, but you raw Highlanders are so darned particular. You can't have it both ways, you know."

"Don't I know it, Sir," laughed Peter. "But you have no idea what a life I would lead if my General heard that I had accepted an officer who was not a Scotsman. He'd send him back on the first available lorry. So I suppose I must just possess my soul in patience."

"I'm afraid that's about what it is, Peter."

"Never mind, Sir. I expect we shall win the battle after all, even without young Douglas. Aren't you lucky to have us Scots to fight the battle for you?"

They both laughed, and started talking about technical subjects.

After a few more minutes, the Signals Colonel rose, said good-bye to his Chief and left the caravan. It was yet early in the day, so he told his driver to leave the Jeep near some other vehicle for safe custody and come and have a swim in the sea. Throughout the campaign they had never missed an opportunity for a bathe. Water was scarce in the Desert, and the usual allowance for each man was only one gallon of water a day for all purposes. This didn't leave a lot

OCTOBER 23rd 1942

for washing, so every swim was worth it many times over.

They both clambered over the sand dunes and down to the water's edge. It was a lovely day, if a trifle warm. Overhead many aeroplanes were zooming their way in the direction of the German lines, but as yet there had been no sign of the Luftwaffe. Peter always hoped that they wouldn't come over, machine-gunning while he was having a swim. It would be rather unpleasant, he thought, to be shot when you hadn't any clothes on.

No enemy planes came over this morning, and they were left to enjoy their bathe undisturbed. What a contrast! A few miles away thousands of men were lying hidden in little slits in the ground, all ready for the great advance of the night, while here was Peter and his driver swimming contentedly in the sea, for all the world as if they were on their summer holidays. It was a mental relief, too; for every time you took your clothes off and entered the sea, you left the war behind you and were back in the days of peace. Every soldier of the Desert Army who has bathed in the cooling waters of the Mediterranean will know just exactly what I mean.

Reluctantly, they got out of the sea and back into the little Jeep for the return journey to Divisional Headquarters.

At seven in the evening, the Colonel was having dinner in 'A' Mess. There was the General, his A.D.C., the G1, the ADMS, the Chief Engineer Officer and the senior officer of the Administrative Services, up for a visit from Rear Headquarters. It was a strange dinner, for they all talked of every subject under the sun, except the battle which was due to start in three hours' time. In a little while, the General would leave for his Battle Headquarters, where Alec Foster was waiting to receive him with a young forest of telephones and wireless sets. But they did not talk of the war, it was too near to them.

The Senior Artillery officer, known as the CRA, came in a bit late.

"Sorry to be late, Sir," he murmured to the General as he sat down.

"You're not late, George," said the G.O.C. "We're a bit early."

"Anything on the news, Master Twiddler?" The CRA turned towards the Signals Colonel.

"I resent the noble title, Sir," laughed Peter. "But since you ask, Mr. Bruce Belfridge has seen fit to announce that in the Western Desert there is nothing to report, and patrol activity continues."

"I wonder what he'll have to announce to-morrow," said the G1.

"Nothing at all, I should think," replied the Doctor. "It will take at least three days for the B.B.C. to hear about our doings out here."

"I smell a dig at Signals there, Sir," laughed Peter.

"Don't be self-conscious about your Signals, Peter," smiled the General. "By the way, have you heard from your uncle lately?"

"I heard just the other day, Sir. He is up at Aberlour having the time of his life fishing the Spey."

"After the war, I'm going to take two months leave and fish all up the North of Scotland," said the General, leaning back in his chair. "After the war, — what a nice thought that is."

"I'm going to take a golfing holiday with James Greig," announced Peter.

"You and your golf," jeered the G 1. "A really good pub-crawl in a big way is much more in your line, if I know anything about it."

Peter laughed. They were always chaffing him, as by far the youngest member of the Mess. "All right, Eric," he smiled back at the G 1 across the table. "Wouldn't you like to come with me ? But I expect your wife would have to say quite a lot about it, wouldn't she ?"

"We'll have to do something about a wife for you, Peter," said the General. "A wealthy bachelor like you just can't be allowed."

"Then you'll all have to rally round and find me what I've been looking for all these years, Sir," smiled Peter, lighting a cigarette.

"What's that, Peter ?" asked the General.

"A really wealthy widow with a hard-working son."

They all laughed, and the mess waiter came in with coffee.

Thus did they laugh and joke with each other, and thus did all officers and other ranks of that great Army laugh and joke with each other on the eve of the Battle of El Alamein. It is not good that soldiers should talk for ever about the difficulties and dangers which lie ahead. These are plain enough for all to see and realise. So, in their off-duty moments, they all avoided conversation about the war, and reverted to the banter and cross-talk of the peacetime mess-table.

After dark in the evening, the Signals Colonel strolled out, on to the road, to see what was to be seen. There was an unearthly hush over the earth, and no vehicles were passing along the roadway in either direction. It would be silent until the barrage opened up at ten o'clock.

Then, from out of the darkness came the sound of the bagpipes. A piper a long way off was playing for his mess-mates. It was a still night, and the wail of the pipes came drifting clear and distinct over the Desert, much the same as it does across the heather moors of far off Scotland. The piper was playing 'Hieland Laddie', and Peter felt the old tune fairly catch him by the throat. He stood quite still and listened. The old martial music of Scotland was preparing her sons for battle, as ever it had been in the days of old. Scotsmen, all the world over, thrill to the song of the pipes, and here, in Africa, many thousands of Scotsmen were listening to these same tunes of their Homeland. The old fighting spirit was still there, a hundred fold. It was not for nothing that the General had issued his Order of the Day as being:

'Scotland for ever, and second to none'.

There would be many a German and Italian who would be sorry he had ever lived to hear that skirl of the bagpipes. The men of Scotland were ready.

CHAPTER IV

BATTLE

For the tenth time in the last three minutes, Lieutenant John Gray of the Inverness Regiment looked at his wrist-watch. The hands still said a quarter past nine, and the battalion was not due to move up to the Start Line until half past. They were sitting down in the Assembly Area whence they had come after their evening meal. John's Company was in the right lead, and the men were sitting or lying about on the sand and rocks of a small hollow, well in front of the gun positions. The moon was full, and it was possible to see quite a long way.

John got to his feet and climbed to the lip of his hollow to have a look around. On either side of his own unit he could see men standing or sitting on the ground. There were very few vehicles, and he could hardly hear any engines running. All vehicles, except those actually needed by the leading troops, were kept a short way back until the Engineers had managed to make gaps in the enemy mine-fields, through which they could pass.

Men were gathered in little groups, talking about what was to happen. Officers flitted here and there, seeing that all the hundred and one details of preparation were complete, right down to the last item. Sitting a few yards from his own platoon was a small party of Sappers with their curious-looking 'Warming pans', long sticks with a round electrical device at the end to detect the presence of enemy mines. The Sapper sergeant was arranging some reels of white tape, carried by three of his men. This tape was to be used to mark the edges of the gaps which his party were to clear.

Once more John looked at his watch. It was five minutes to the half hour. He went back to his platoon and gave the order to fall in. The men got to their feet and formed into single files of sections. On their left and behind them, other platoons were doing the same. John's platoon was the right hand one of the right leading company. Major Wilson came up to John.

"Ready, old son?"

"All present and correct, Sir."

The Major looked at his watch. "I make it half a minute to go," he said. "What do you say?"

"Same as you, Sir."

The Company on their left started to move forward. "Come on, we're off." So saying, the Major moved off to walk with his Company Headquarters, leaving John to lead his platoon straight ahead towards the Start Line.

They filed out from the small depression they had been resting in and on into the open desert. As yet there were no guns firing, for the barrage was not due to begin until ten o'clock. By that time the leading infantry would be through our own mine-field and crossing the Start Line several hundreds of yards beyond. There were no shells coming over from the direction of the German lines. The enemy had not yet spotted anything amiss.

Young John Gray walked along, with his runner beside him and his sergeant just behind. After the sergeant came the platoon in single file by sections, but the men were not covering off each other, in order to avoid too many of them being hit by the same bullet. It was an eerie sight, these columns of infantrymen steadily walking forward across the sands under the brilliant tropical moon, with hardly a sound to give away the fact that they were there at all.

Two lights a short way ahead denoted the first gap, which was in the British minefield. These lamps had been placed on the outer edges of the gap, and underneath one of the lamps was a small notice board on which was written 'Gap No.1'. John could see other small lights away to his left, marking the other gaps through which 'B' and 'C' Companies would pass. As he entered his own gap, he could clearly see the lines of white tape put there by the Sappers. These tapes marked the limits of safe ground. To put one foot outside was to ask to be blown up by a mine.

The minefield was about fifty yards long, and just as John was nearly at the other side, there was a familiar hiss and whine in the air overhead. A shell landed about a hundred yards to his right rear. The crash of the explosion sounded apallingly loud in the silence of the night. Another and another shell came over and the cracks of the high explosive got nearer and nearer to their gap. But still the men plodded steadily forward. It was no use at all to stop, especially in the middle of a minefield gap. The Bosche always shelled these gaps as soon as he discovered that they had been made. They were in full view of the enemy, but his foremost line was still a couple of miles away, so observation in that deceptive moonlight could not be any too good.

It is surprising how near to you a shell can land without doing any damage. The noise is what is most disconcerting. You can hear the beastly thing coming a long way off, just like an express train running into a cutting. But there is very little you can do about it. If you are on a job where you can duck into a hollow or slit-trench, that is certainly the best place to be; but if you are taking part in an infantry advance, you can only continue walking straight ahead and hope to goodness that your name isn't on any of the shells.

John Gray's platoon was just clear of the minefield gap when a shell landed fair and square in the clearance behind the last man. There was a piercing scream in the darkness, followed by a voice shouting in agony. "God damn you, you bastards, you've blown my bloody arm off! Christ! What a mess!" His voice trailed off into mere groans.

"See who that was, Sergeant Jackson," said John. His knees were shaking a little, but he hoped none of his men noticed it.

"All right, Sir. I'll make up on you in a wee while." The sergeant dropped back to see who had been hit. Two stretcher bearers were bending over the wounded man and a couple of Jocks were standing by, looking rather sick.

"Come along there," Sergeant Jackson said. "You can't do anything here, so off you go after the others. These medical lads will look after him."

"It's ma freen, Sairgint," replied one of the two. "Can ah no bide wie 'im for a bittie?"

"Sorry, laddie. There'll be many more like him before this night is out. So you'd better be getting along. Come on, we'll go together." He started to walk quickly in the direction of the fast disappearing platoon.

"Bad luck, sonnie." The sergeant patted the Jock who had lost his friend on the arm. "But if all stayed back to look after him, there'd be precious few left to fight the Jerries."

"Dinna fear aboot me, Sairgint," muttered the man fiercely. "I'll finish off a few of the swine for this."

"That's the stuff, lad," said Jackson, and left him with his pal as they drew level with their Section.

"Who was it?" asked John Gray, as the sergeant came up with him.

"Macdonald, Sir, the fellow who was your batman for a couple of weeks on the boat."

"Is he bad?"

"Stopped a nasty one on the left arm, Sir. Looks pretty bad; it was only hanging by a shred. There are two orderlies looking after him. He'll be all right when they get him back to the Dressing Station."

But he didn't get back to the Dressing Station. He died a couple of minutes after Sergeant Jackson had passed on with the two Jocks. Poor Macdonald, he never had a chance to hit out at a German. He it was who had been sharpening his bayonet two days before, and had said that he would give them "That for Paisley, and That for Clydebank, and That for ma faither in the last war".

Never mind Mac, there's many of your pals who will avenge your death this night.

The shells were falling fairly thick and fast as they approached the Start Line, but surprisingly few men had been hit so far. John Gray looked at his watch. It was one minute to ten, the guns were about to open fire. A white line on the ground at his feet told him that he was crossing the Start Line. He passed over it with a queer thrill in his bones.

The Battle of Alamein had begun.

Suddenly there was a brilliant flash lighting up the whole sky, followed by a rumble as of a great thunderstorm. Ahead of the advancing troops a line of fire broke out all along the enemy front. Crash after crash burst into the stillness of the night. There was silence no longer, the guns had opened up what was to be the greatest barrage the British Army had ever attempted since the War of 1914-18.

John Gray had seen artillery fire before. But this was far more intense than he could have imagined in his wildest dreams. Away in front of him brilliant flashes flickered from right to left and back again. The noise was deafening. The whole earth seemed to shake and heave to the tune of this terrible orchestra.

He continued to walk forward, but in a kind of stupor. This noise deadened the senses ; it was stupendous.

"I'll bet Jerry doesn't like that, Sir." It was Sergeant Jackson's voice at his elbow. The sound of another human being brought him back to earth. He laughed.

"Isn't it grand ?"

"Aye, Sir. We're beginning to get a little bit of our own back from what happened at St. Valerie."

"About time too."

The thin lines of men continued to stream steadily forward in the wake of the shells. The General had often said that there was no place quite as safe as right up behind your own barrage. Young John Gray was finding now how true those words were. The German shells were passing overhead and bursting a safe way behind the attacking troops. For several hundreds of yards no man of the Inverness Regiment had been hit. John saw his Company Commander walking steadily forward, his runner striding along beside him. Major Wilson looked for all the world as if he were walking up one of his own broad grouse moors back in Scotland. Behind him came his company piper, playing the Regimental march of 'Hieland Laddie'. Above the noise of the guns and the screaming of the enemy shells the skirl of the pipes was plainly audible. Every man of that company walked with his head a little higher because he heard that tune lilting away ahead of him. It would be a tragedy indeed if the company piper should be hit by a stray bullet.

There are those who laugh at the music of the bagpipes, and who maintain that it is a barbarous sound.

But let them march behind a piper into battle and reconsider their ideas. To the men of Scotland, walking across the sands of the Western Desert into the teeth of murderous machine-gun fire and across unseen minefields, the tune of their native pipes acted as a great tonic and inspiration.

On the morning after the battle, a Subaltern of the Signal Service came upon a piper of the Blach Watch. He was lying dead across the enemy wire — but his pipes were still between his teeth.

These pipers of the Highland Division did more than they can ever know in that great battle of Alamein. They carried the men of the Division forward to the sound of the old battle songs of Scotland, and they carried them to a great victory.

At long last the first enemy minefield was reached, where the ever faithful Sappers had prepared a gap. Sure enough, John could see the lights marking the boundaries of the pathway through which it was now safe to proceed. But as he passed through it, he could see several dim shapes lying on either side, shapes which were the bodies of men of the Royal Engineers who had died in making this gap for the infantry. And more than the infantry, — if these gaps did not exist, no vehicles or tanks could ever move forward. John remembered that behind the Highland Division there waited a great formation of armoured fighting tanks waiting for the anti-tank mines to be removed.

At the next minefield there would be no waiting Sappers with their friendly gap. It was too far in front to expect even these brave men to penetrate without the protecting screen of infantry to assist them. John and his platoon would have to go on and take their chance of getting through alive before they could get at the enemy on the far side.

The enemy machine-guns were beginning to take a toll of the Inverness Regiment, and many a Jock sank to the ground, quivering, when a German bullet found its deadly mark. John went on untouched amid the hail of bullets, until the battalion reached the place where they were to make a pause of a quarter of an hour. It was in a little hollow in the ground, and the men fell flat on their faces, thankful of the short respite.

"Are you all right, John ?" It was Major Wilson who spoke.

"Quite all right, Sir," answered John with a smile, as he lit a cigarette. "Like one, Sir ?"

"Thanks." The two officers lay there silently for a few moments.

"Lost many chaps ?" asked the Major at length.

"Eleven. Not as bad as I had expected."

"It's never as bad as you think it is going to be, old son. I can remember in France when we were retreating towards St. Valerie. I never imagined that any of us could possibly get away alive. And nearly half a brigade managed to get out unscathed. It can always be worse."

"I suppose it can, Sir," smiled John. There was a sudden whine in the air above them, and both officers buried their faces in the sand. About twenty yards away there was a tremendous explosion. John felt the hot blast tearing at his thin shorts and shirt.

"Are you all right, John?"

"O.K., thanks, Sir. And you?"

"Old soldiers never die." They both laughed.

"Well, I must be getting along. See you at the objective, John." With that, the Major left him to his own thoughts. He got to his feet and made his way down the ranks of his platoon. With a cheery word here and there he endeavoured to keep their spirits up. All that they wanted was to come to grips with the enemy who was giving them such a bad time.

"Let's get on at them, Sorr," was the remark he heard on all sides.

"All right, lads," he smiled back. "Bide a wee and we'll be going on. It won't be long now, never fear."

Almost before he expected it, the whistle went, and they were once more walking steadily forward in the direction of the enemy. They came to the next minefield. John felt a little nervous as he set foot on the far side of the wire. At any moment he might be blown to pieces, and he picked his steps carefully. A few paces on, and one of his platoon stepped on a mine. There was a small explosion and a black object sprang up into the air.

"Down!" shouted John. But it was too late. There was a sharp crack and the anti-personnel mine exploded, blowing the man's chest in, leaving his body writhing on the ground. There was nothing they could do, so the rest of the platoon continued on their way through that murderous minefield. Men were falling on either side as they emerged at the other end. John caught a glimpse of field-grey ahead. It was the long sought enemy.

"At them, lads!" he shouted. And the whole platoon surged forward with their bayonets glistening in the moonlight.

John never realised clearly what happened during the next few minutes. There were screams in the darkness and terrible sounds of worrying. Grey shapes and khaki shapes kept flickering into his vision and out of it again. Men lunged at each other with bayonets and rolled on the sands with their hands at each others throats. The screams of the mortally hit and the groans of the wounded made a dreadful sound. He saw Sergeant Jackson fell a huge German officer with the butt of his rifle. One moment the officer was towering above him, and the next he was lying on the sand with his head battered in. His servant chased an Italian corporal for several yards before he managed to get his bayonet well and truly into him, when the man went down with a dreadful scream.

John saw many terrible things which he would never forget, and then, quite suddenly, the scene cleared, and there were no Germans or Italians left. They were either dead or had run away, leaving the men of the Inverness Regiment in undisputed ownership of the situation.

"Dig, you fellows! Dig like blazes!" It was Major Wilson who had spoken. He was standing in front of John and his platoon.

"Dig like hell!" he urged. "There will almost certainly be a counter attack, and if they use tanks you will want to be in decent slit trenches. So dig for your very lives. We've jolly well got to hold this place now that we've got it."

So they dug, every man where he stood. And after half an hour they had got the place in a pretty decent state of defence. But there was no counter attack. In the dim light of the dawn, after the artillery barrage had ceased, there was only one sound which came lilting across the desert wastes, the sound of the bagpipes. The men of Scotland had triumphed again.

CHAPTER V

DOGFIGHT

JOHN GRAY, SUBALTERN OF THE INVERNESS Regiment, lay in a small scrape in the sand and hoped for the best. It was not yet light, but the artillery barrage had ceased altogether. The absence of sound was much more frightening than the awful din which had gone on all through the night. A few rifle shots went off occasionally into the darkness, but of heavy gun-fire there was none.

His company was spread out on a small hill, and his platoon was the foremost of the company. 'B' Company was a couple of hundred yards away to John's left, and he could see a few tin hats sticking up dimly above the ground level in the greyness of the approaching light. Gradually it got lighter, and he looked about him to see what he could before the enemy started to take notice.

His platoon had dug itself in on the forward slopes of the little hill. It couldn't really be called a hill, it was nothing more than a piece of rising ground But it gave quite a decent view in the direction of the enemy. About a hundred yards away to John's right rear were the remains of one of the battalion carriers. It had been struck fair and square by a shell from a field gun, and was lying there smouldering, just a heap of twisted metal. What had happened to the men who had been in it, he did not know. In all probability they lay somewhere in that burning mass — or at least, what was left of them.

His Sergeant had sited a light machine-gun post just on his right, but as yet it had not opened fire — there was nothing to fire at. The men were lying in their trenches, endeavouring to make them a little deeper before it was too light to show a man's body above the surface of the sand. John and his platoon well knew that if the tanks did not come through now, they would be pinned here all day until at last a kindly darkness descended upon the earth once more. It would be fatal to show above the level of the sand, and as they were lying on the forward slopes of the hill, there would be no movement during the hours of daylight.

John got out his field-glasses and took a look to his front. He couldn't see much at first, owing to the morning haze. But after a few minutes things cleared. There would be good visibility until the sun had got well up and the usual desert mirrage settled upon the sands.

He could see about a mile, or a mile and a half. There were a few bodies lying about, both German and British. None of these gave the slightest sign of movement, so John concluded that they were all dead. It would be unpleasant if they had been alive, for it was quite impossible to go out and bring them in before it was dark again. Two German tanks stood out against the desert, great hulks of metal, with smoke coming out of them on all sides. One had the body of a man, naked as he was born, lying half out of the turret. The force of an explosion must have ripped the clothes off his body.

John shuddered. What a rotten thing war was!

Suddenly he stiffened. Peering through his glasses he saw what he had been seeking for. Away on the far horizon, just a mere speck, or so it seemed at first, he saw something move. He looked more closely, and saw that it was the head of an enemy soldier. The man was lying on the ground and peering through glasses. John knew what that meant. If the German detected the British position, mortar shells would come dropping round them before they knew where they were.

John slid back into his trench in the sand and raised his voice for his platoon to hear.

"Lie flat, all of you. Each Section will detail two men to keep a look-out. The rest of you will try to get some sleep. Be careful with your rations, don't eat them all up at once. You never know when we'll get any more. We're probably here till darkness at least. No man is to show himself above the level of the ground."

There were a few answering cries of "Right you are, Sir," and John settled down to try to eat some sandwiches. It was the queerest picnic he had ever attended. But the food put new life into him, and he began to hope that perhaps the tanks would come through before the end of the morning and save them that awful wait through the heat of the day.

They lay there for perhaps another two hours when the fun started without any warning whatsoever.

There was a sudden whistle in the air above the platoon a little way in front of them. John awoke from his doze with a start, just as a mortar shell crashed into the sand a hundred yards in front of their position. It was followed quickly by another and another, all of them falling short of where the Inverness lads were lying. Then, again without warning, the Germans lengthened their range, and the next few shells fell right in the middle of the platoon position. The noise was most unpleasant, and only those who have been shelled by mortars at close range can ever imagine just how unpleasant it is. Probably it is the worst thing that can happen to any soldier in a war. Mortar shelling is by far the most frightening of the lot. They make a dreadful *'Crack'* as they land, and every single one is coming straight for *you* ; or so it feels to every soldier in the position which is being shelled.

John lay still in his slit and prayed. His platoon lay and prayed and sweated also. There wasn't a man who wasn't chewing the sand, and liking it ! It's no use saying that they weren't frightened. They all were, every man of them. The man who isn't frightened when he is being shelled by mortars at close range just doesn't exist, except in story books, and bad story books at that.

These men had marched steadily into the teeth of enemy machine-gun fire all the previous night. They had met the enemy on his own ground, and had beaten him, beaten him hollow. They had sent those Germans running for their lives, with a very wholesome respect for Highland steel.

But this was a different kettle of fish. It is one thing to advance with your comrades against the enemy when the blood is up, especially if your Company Piper is playing a stirring tune. You have company, and the battle is on. There is a barrage over your head, and you are advancing behind your own guns. There is every chance of being able to come to grips with a very human enemy at the end of the proceedings. But when you are lying in a slit in the ground, when they start shelling you with mortar fire, when you'll be greeted with a hail of bullets, if you as much as show your head above the level of the earth — that is a very different thing. It is then that every man is alone, in a small world by himself. He has no other man to talk to. He cannot hear the stirring tune of the pipes. All he hears is the whistle and whine of those shells, coming, he is certain, straight for *him*. This is not the time to give it, it is the time to take it. These Jocks could take it, but it was a very unpleasant experience.

The shelling went on for nearly three hours. Surprisingly few of the men in John's platoon were hit. One shell landed directly in the slit-trench next to his own. There was no sound from the man in it. John knew that it was no use getting up to see if by chance there was anything left of the poor fellow. He knew that there would not be, and he would only throw away his own life in the effort.

At one time a man lost his nerve and started screaming. "Christ! Stop this noise! I can't stand any more of it!"

"Stop it, lad! Stop it at once!" shouted the Sergeant, and the boy subsided into low mutterings.

But for the most part these sturdy Jocks stood the strain very well indeed. Their turn would come again to go out after the enemy, but for the moment there was nothing else to do but to lie low and hope for the best. After three hours of it, our own field guns opened up. After some ten minutes of intense shelling on the enemy position, the mortar team was silenced, and John's platoon was left in peace to pull their scattered wits together and get a little sleep.

Evidently the tanks were *not* coming through that day. But John offered up a silent prayer of thanks to some ever-watchful Gunner Officer who had spotted the position of that enemy mortar emplacement, had brought his guns to bear upon it, and so relieved their torment.

All through the long, hot afternoon, they lay there. Each man occupied with his own thoughts, and all trying to snatch a few hours sleep, in readiness for the inevitable advance which must take place when once again darkness had fallen on the earth. It was not till after dusk that any of them dared to move out of his hole in the ground.

As soon as it was quite dark, food started to come up for the troops holding the front. A runner crawled up to John Gray's trench to bring him a message from the Company Commander. It was to the effect that he was to send his men back in small parties at a time, to a place just behind the small hill in rear of their position. Here the platoon would get food in relays.

The men were to crawl, for the enemy might well be able to see a man walking in the moonlight. John himself was to come back to Company Headquarters for orders.

He called to his Sergeant and made arrangements for all the men to get back in their turn for the evening meal, and then he crawled away himself to look for the Company Commander, not daring to stand up till he was well below the sky-line at the other side of the hill. After looking round for a few minutes, he located the place where several of the other officers of his Company were seated on the ground round the Major. They were all eating out of their mess-tins, and drinking mugs of steaming tea. A short distance away a couple of cooks were dishing out food for the men from three large dixies.

John sat down in the little group of officers and his servant went off to get him his meal.

"Now we're all here," the Company Commander said, "I'll tell you what the Colonel told me half an hour ago. We've got to hang on here for another night and day, as we can't advance until to-morrow night. The Australians on our right are putting in an attack to-night, and all our artillery is being used to help them on. A hell of a lot of other guns are firing as well, so we can't expect any firing on our own front. The tanks didn't get through anywhere last night. They ran into a lot of mines all over the place, and we didn't get on quite as fast as we had hoped to.

"The Army Commander said that there would probably be a dog-fight of anything up to a week before the Bosche finally broke. So we mustn't be disappointed if we don't beat them in one night's fighting."

"Once the Australians have captured their objective of to-night, the high ground overlooking our present position, then there is a good chance that the Armoured Boys may be able to come through. But until the Poor Blessed Infantry have lifted all the mines in front of them, the tanks just haven't a chance of doing anything at all."

"But there's one thing which ought to cheer you all up. The Gunners have managed to get a lot of anti-tank guns up just behind us here. In fact, if you look over there" — and he pointed over his left shoulder — "you'll be able to see where some of them are. So if we get counter-attacked by the Bosche tanks, I don't think we've got anything much to be afraid of. Just tell your chaps to stop in their slit-trenches till after the tanks have passed over them, and then to bob up and have a pot shot at them. But for the Lord's sake be careful not to shoot up the anti-tank guns over there. They won't thank you any if you do. If they are firing at the time, I would strongly advise you to lie low, unless there are any infantry coming along with the tanks."

"You are all doing frightfully well, and I want you to keep a look-out for any names for decorations after this little show is finished. I'll call for them later on, when the battle's over. — My God! This tea tastes like salty water! I'd give a lot for a nice, cool whisky and soda."

"Major Wilson!" A voice called out of the semi-darkness.

"Over here; who wants me?"

"All right, we'll come over to you." Two figures approached the little group of officers. One was Forsyth, the Colonel of the Regiment, and beside him stood a very tall and thin officer wearing a balmoral bonnet, shirt and shorts, and the usual cross-straps of webbing which supported a revolver and a large pair of field-glasses. There was no mistaking those clear, deepset eyes and the drooping moustache. The officers scrambled hastily to their feet. It was the GOC commanding their Division.

"For goodness sake sit down," he said. "You'll want all the rest you can get. How are you all? Getting a good meal, I see."

"All in good heart, Sir," smiled Major Wilson. "We're just having a Company Officers' conference, and I'm giving them the dope as far as I know it. The Jocks are having their meal in relays."

"Well done, that's good, Wilson. Now take me to where I can see your Company front. I want to have a look at it. Where shall we go?"

"Up to the top of that small hill, Sir. You'll be able to see it all from there. But you'd better lie down when you get near the top. Shall I lead the way?"

"Go on, I'll follow," said the General, and both officers walked away, followed by the Colonel. When they got near the top of the rising ground, all three got down to it and crawled the last few yards. At the top, the General lay beside the Company Commander and peered ahead into the moonlight in the direction of the German lines. They stayed there for a full quarter of an hour while the GOC took in every detail of the situation. He was very much a Frontline soldier, and had spent the last hour visiting several forward companies along the Divisional front.

Eventually the little party came down from their point of vantage, and the GOC went across to where some of the men were eating their meal. He chatted away to several of them, before he said good-bye, and left the vicinity with the Colonel.

"I never thought Generals ever came as far forward as this," said John Gray, as they sat down again.

"Then you thought wrong, my son," laughed his Company Commander. "How do you think a General could command at all if he never went up to have a look at the ground for himself?"

"Can't he depend on messages coming in?"

"And act on information several hours late? Not on your life, young John. A Commander nowadays has got to study the ground even more than ever before, and he can never do that entirely from a map. Do you know that there has been an argument as to our own position here? Some chaps go so far as to say we are two thousand yards more to the right than we actually are. There's map reading for you! No, my lad. When you're a General, which Heaven forbid, you'll see all you want to of the front line. All those stories of Generals sitting back, well out of range of shot and shell, are all my eye."

"It's time you chaps were getting back to your troops. But I want you here at nine o'clock sharp, I'll be able to give you any orders for patrolling. We're bound to have to do a spot of patrol work to-night, so you'd better be ready for it. Off you go."

The officers got up and went back to their platoons.

At nine o'clock, nothing much had happened beside a few desultory shells, and John Gray found himself once more listening to his Company Commander speaking about the night's patrols.

"John," said Major Wilson, "I want you to take out a dozen men yourself and try to find out what happened to that mortar position which was shelling us this afternoon. The Brigadier thinks that they may have set up another somewhere nearby the same place. Don't get too much involved, as I don't particularly want to lose you. But try to find out if there is another mortar there by now. If there is, we'll get the Gunners to shell it just after dawn to-morrow."

"When do I start, Sir?" asked John.

"Better not go out before three, as the moon will be about setting by then. Also the Australian show will be over before that."

"Right you are, Sir."

"The password will be 'Aberlour'. Just to give a touch of old Scotland. I'll bet no Bosche could pronounce that as it should be spoken. Off you go, to your platoons."

The meeting broke off, and John went back to his men on the forward slopes of the hill. He called his sergeant and fixed up who should be with him on the patrol, then he went to his slit-trench to get what sleep he could before he started out on his adventure in No Man's Land.

Patrols are the very devil. You never know what is going to happen. Sometimes you will go out and nothing at all happens. You prowl around trying to find out all you can about some part of the enemy's position, and you see absolutely nothing. But on other occasions just everything happens. You run into a patrol of the enemy, and you either get wiped out, or you have a merry little scrap and the whole world joins in. Then you find that every soldier in the vicinity lets fly with every weapon he can lay his hands on, and the earth becomes a most unpleasant place. You are darned lucky if you ever get back to your own lines. It often depends on such little things as a sneeze at the wrong moment, or an enemy sentry putting up a flare when a man is moving who ought to have been lying down.

John Gray knew quite a lot about patrols. He had done two when his Brigade had been in the line in the preparatory period of training behind El Amayid. He had been new to the job then, and it had all seemed like a game. But it was different now; he and his men had tasted battle experience, and he knew exactly what he was in for. Still, there was no earthly use worrying about it — what must be, must be. He told his servant to wake him at half past two in the morning and settled down to sleep. There were very few shells coming over from the enemy lines, and he soon dozed off into an untroubled sleep.

He had hardly closed his eyes, or so it seemed to him, when he was awakened by his batman shaking his shoulder.

"It's half past two, Sir. You asked to be called at half past two."

"Right you are," said John sleepily, heaving himself up out of his trench. The moon was hanging very low in the sky, and there was a complete silence over the desert. No guns were firing, and not even the odd rifle was letting fly. German and Britisher were holding their peace. Sergeant Jackson came up out of the darkness. "I've wakened the patrol, Sir," he said. "They'll all be ready in fifteen minutes."

"Well done, good and faithful one," grinned John. "But I don't know so much about the 'Joy of thy Lord'. I was having such a lovely sleep."

"I wish I was back in bed with the wife, Sir. These early mornings get me down. Except when I'm going out fishing."

"You and your fishing, I don't believe you ever caught anything in the hours of darkness. Now did you?"

"More than you'd ever believe, Sir."

"You fishermen are all the same," said John, getting into his webbing equipment. "Help me on with this monstrosity, will you, there's a good chap."

They both struggled with the jigsaw puzzle, and at last the young officer was properly dressed for war. Some day, an inspired Staff will design a reasonable dress for its soldiers to fight in. From time immemorial the wretched soldier has been sent into battle with everything but the kitchen stove wrapped round his person. But John had learned his lesson in the bitter school of experience, and he only wore what was absolutely necessary. He carried his revolver, field-glasses and pouch of ammunition. That was all, or nearly all. For in his stocking leg he had a wicked looking little knife. Not the ordinary dirk of the Highland Regiments of Scotland, but a lethal weapon he had purchased in a weak moment in London before he had sailed. He maintained that the knife was a darned sight more silent than the revolver when it came to close range work.

"Call the men together, I want to speak to them before we start."

"Right you are, Sir." The Sergeant melted away into the night.

He returned after a few minutes with ten men of the platoon, headed by one Sergeant Tyers, who commanded one of the sections. Sergeant Tyers was in private life a garage hand in Aberdeen, and an amateur boxer of note into the bargain. The remainder of the men were just plain, ordinary, honest-to-God Jocks. The kind that the Germans in the Great War of 1914-18 called the 'Ladies from Hell', because they wore the kilt and would as soon stick a bayonet in a German as hear him shout 'Kamerad'.

"Sit down," said John Gray, and the men sat down around him in a small semicircle.

"Well, chaps," he went on. "We've a pretty decent job to do to-night. I'll lead the way, but if anything happens to me, each one of you must know what the object of this patrol is, so that he can carry on if the worst happens and we are seen by the Bosche. We are to go out and have a look round that mortar emplacement that gave us such a bad time this afternoon. The Powers that Be think that Jerry may have sited another mortar near to the same place, and we are to try to find out if it's true. If there is, we shall do our best to do it in. If there isn't, well, we'll bring back news that there's nothing there after all. Is that clear to you all?"

A chorus of "Aye, Sir" came back from the darkness. These Jocks knew full well what they had to do, and there would be no fear but that they would each and every one of them do his best to carry it out.

"On then, my merry men," said John, getting to his feet. "Follow me in single file, and for the Lord's sake don't any one of you sneeze."

They filed out into the darkness, John leading the way, followed closely by Sergeant Tyers and the rest of the ten men. Their feet made no sound in the soft sand. The moon had set, and there was only very little light. John peered in front of him, but he could see very little in the dim darkness.

For about a mile they carried on with nothing to stop or hinder them. Not a sound was to be heard across the desert. No gun fired, and no German saw fit to unload his rifle into the darkness. John was counting his paces, and he reckoned that he must be about four hundred yards from the place the mortar had been. He signalled for the patrol to stop, and crept near to Sergeant Tyers. Cupping his hands near to the Sergeant's ear, he whispered: "I'm going on ahead to see what I can. Keep the men here and don't move till I come back."

"O.K., Sir," whispered the Sergeant with a nod, and John melted away into the night.

His heart felt about the region of his boots, but the job had to be done, and the sooner he got the information he had come out for the sooner he would be able to return to his Company and his slit-trench. He had come to look upon that slit-trench as his home, in this desert. There he would be free to sleep, whilst out here he had to creep on his stomach and look out for Germans. What a life!

What was that? About a hundred yards ahead there was a dark shape which looked like one of the low bushes which were pretty common in this part of the desert. He lay quite still. He wasn't sure, but he thought he had seen something move near that bush. Every single shadow helds a German when you are out on patrol, and John well knew the necessity of not letting his nerves get the better of him. He peered out into the darkness. Yes, the bush *had* moved, there was no doubt about it, and there was no wind. The night was as still as death.

He wriggled ever so slowly away to the left, trying to get a side view of this bush, but it seemed to him ages before he could get near enough to see without being seen. He was about fifty yards from the spot he was watching, when he saw a man's figure get to his feet from the middle of the bush, as it were, and make off into the darkness. There were thin clouds over the face of the moon, and it was difficult to see with any accuracy what was happening in front of him. The man disappeared from view, and there seemed to be no other enemy in the vicinity. But this illusion was quickly dispelled, for suddenly there was a sound of voices from the dark blotch ahead of where he lay. He couldn't make out what they were saying, and even if he had been able to do so, John's German was very much of the schoolboy variety. But of one thing he was certain, it was German voices which he heard, and there were not more than four of them. Here was a chance for his patrol to grab a prisoner. He had not been told to bring one in, but surely an identification would be valuable to the General Staff!

He slid carefully back to where he had left the rest of his patrol. Quickly he explained his plan in whispers to each of the men. Four of them were to remain where they were to give covering fire, if needed. The remaining six were to spread out, three on either side of the bush, and a concerted rush was to be made on a signal from John, who would be in the lead. One man was detailed to grab the prisoner and bring him back to the waiting four. Everything was to be done as silently as possible. Only knives and bayonets were to be used, and no shots would be fired unless it was absolutely necessary.

A few minutes later, they were lying up some twenty five yards from the place where John had heard the voices. There was a complete hush over the desert, not a sound was to be heard. No voices came from the clump of bushes, all was as still as the dead.

John signalled the other six to get to their feet, and they all moved rapidly and silently across the short piece of intervening ground to the place where the Germans were lying. As John came up to it, he saw immediately what it was. A fairly deep pit, about ten feet all round, and in the middle stood a fair sized trench mortar. Four men lay there, obviously asleep, or nearly so, two on each side of the piece. They must have been lying with their eyes closed, for none of them moved, even when John and his six Jocks arrived over the brim of the pit. All six leaped down on top of the resting men. There was a horrible sound as of worrying, and one stifled scream. That was all. Two of the Jocks heaved a struggling form on to the parapet of the pit where a third gave him a heavy blow on the head with the butt of his rifle. Then they picked up the small, unresisting body of the German and dragged it away in the direction of the British Lines.

John had the presence of mind to tear a set of Regimental badges from one of the three dead Germans, to serve as identifications when he made his report later, and then, hopping lightly out of the trench, he ran like a rabbit to where he had left the other four of his patrol. Flinging himself down to the ground, he tried to regain his breath. Would the enemy have heard what they had been doing ? At any moment he expected a perfect fusilade of fire to come sweeping over the desert, and pin his patrol to the spot for hours, if not for the whole of the following day.

But nothing happened at all. The little raid had been carried out in almost perfect silence, save for that one muffled scream, which evidently nobody had heard. Three Germans would fight no more, and the other one lay tightly held down by two Jocks, and was fast recovering consciousness. He was only a youngster, and looked frightened to death.

"Come on, lads," said John when he had recovered his breath. "Back we go; we've done all we came out for, and more." He led the way back in single file towards the lines of the Inverness Regiment. As they got near, they were challenged with a shout of: "Halt! Who goes there?"

"Aberlour — Gray returning from patrol."

"Advance and be recognised."

John walked slowly forward till the waiting men saw who he was.

"O.K., Sir. Pass, all's well."

John and his men moved on with their captive till they came to the Company Headquarters where they handed him over to be searched before being sent back to Divisional Headquarters.

Major Wilson was waiting for John to hear his report, and he smiled when he heard the story of how his little party had surprised the Bosche mortar team. "That'll learn them to pop shells down on us while we are trying to get a little sleep," he commented. "But you've done jolly well, old son. There's a hot mug of tea for you and your merry men. Go and get it, and then down to some sleep. You never know, but the beggars may try an attack before dawn. I'll tell the Colonel how well you've done. I know how pleased he will be."

John felt suddenly very weary indeed. The strain of the last few hours, and days, was beginning to tell. He must get some sleep if he was to be able to carry on at all. He made his way across to where he could get a mug of hot tea. The hot liquid put new life into him, and things didn't seem too bad. But he must sleep, and at once. So he went forward to his platoon, and sought his own little slit-trench. His Sergeant was waiting for him in the next hole to his.

"How did you get on, Sir?"

"Damned good, Jackson. We found a mortar team and killed three of them. There was another, and we brought him along with us. Pretty good show, eh?"

"As you say, Sir. A pretty good show. I hope you'll get something for this, Sir. The men would be proud if you did."

"All I want now, Sergeant, is a spot of decent sleep. Call me at six, just before it's light, there's a good chap."

"I'll see to that myself, Sir. You go to sleep now."

"Good-night."

"Good-night, Sir. Sleep well."

Almost before John's head had come to rest on his waterproof cape, he was asleep. The moon had set, and utter darkness reigned across the Western Desert. There were no sounds except the occasional snore of a man in a nearby slit-trench.

CHAPTER VI

DON R

It was eleven o'clock on the night of the 24th of October, and the guns were going at it full blast. The Signal Centre was well in front of the gun positions, and the men inside could hear the whine of the shells as they passed overhead. The Australians were putting in an attack, supported by all the artillery which could be brought to bear on their front. Occasionally, there came the dull explosion of German shells landing in the vicinity of the Signal Centre of the Highland Division.

James Thompson was asleep in the little dug-out reserved for those of the Signallers who were lucky enough to be off duty. He had been hard at it all day, delivering despatches in his Jeep. He had only got back from his last run at nine o'clock, and had managed to get a bite of hot food from the cooks, just as they were knocking off for the night. This had put new life into James Thompson, for he had been feeling very tired. Driving a Jeep all day in that heavy sand was a tough job, and several enemy shells had landed far too close to him for his comfort. There was no use getting out and hiding in a slit-trench, always supposing there was one handy. For the messages had to be delivered in the quickest possible time, and no Don R* worthy of the name would be

---
* Despatch Rider

guilty of taking shelter, unless it were absolutely necessary.

James was a butcher in Thurso in private life, and he had joined the Territorial Army when it was duplicated in 1939. He had been called up at the beginning of the War and had served in France with the old 51st Division. He had been very lucky, and had got away with the remnant which was saved from the debacle at St. Valerie.

He wasn't an imaginative sort of a fellow, and the artillery barrage did not keep him awake. Sufficient unto the day were the jobs thereof, and he had got down to it in the little dug-out, well knowing that he would probably be called out before very long, as there were only three other Don R's at TAC Headquarters, besides himself.

He had had a wretched day, and had been sent out to visit all three Infantry Brigades in the Division, not to speak of two of the Artillery Regiments. He had been bombed by Stukas and shelled by field-guns in the course of his travels round the Divisional front. The Desert tracks were none too good for driving along, and his arms ached from fatigue. On the whole, he took rather a gloomy view of the War, and longed for the day when he could be back in his native Thurso, able to spend his evenings in the local pub, and not have to drive a perishing little Jeep across the Libyan Sands, being shot at by every Hun who took a dislike to Scottish Despatch Riders. Not that any German gunner had ever set eyes upon James Thompson, but he himself would swear by all his gods that he was their only target.

He longed for his home in Scotland, and he longed for a glass of cool beer, but he well knew that this could never be until Rommel, and all he stood for, had been driven from the shores of Africa. How that was to be done, James Thompson was well content to leave to more capable hands than his own, and for the moment he was well pleased to be able to lie down and sleep, hoping that his turn to go out would not come before he had had a decent rest.

He lay in his clothes, fully dressed, his tin hat beside him, and his tousled head of curly brown hair resting on his haversack. The fact that this contained his tin mug and mess-tin worried him not a bit. For James Thompson was tired, very tired, and the only thing that mattered at the moment was sleep. All the Gunners in creation weren't going to keep him awake.

At about half-past eleven, James awoke to find one of the Signal Office orderlies bending over him shaking his shoulder.

"What's up?" he asked in a sleepy voice.

"You're wanted at the Signal Office. Job of work for you, Jimmy. I wouldn't be a Don R for all the money in the world."

"You wouldn't know what to do with all the money in the world," retorted James Thompson as he struggled out of his blankets.

"I'd soon have some beer sent up here, anyway," remarked the orderly as he left the dug-out with James.

They walked the two hundred yards to the Signal Office where James went in to see the Sergeant in charge.

"Run for you, Thompson," said the Sergeant as soon as he saw him.

"Where to, Sergeant?" asked James.

"123 Brigade. You know where they are?"

"I'll say I do. I've been there three times already to-day. They'll attach me to their Signal Section if I go there again."

"Here's your docket*. Don't lose it, and bring back a receipt with you. And you might as well take these letters for Mr. Mackay as you are going there in any case."

"Right you are, Sergeant. Anything more?"

"No. Off you go. Look out for the minefields. We can't afford to lose any more Jeeps."

"I notice you don't mention Don R's, Sergeant," grinned James.

"Outside," laughed the Sergeant, and turned back to his work.

James adjusted his tin hat and made his way to his Jeep. The sky was lit up with the flashes of guns and the noise of the barrage was almost deafening. The Australian attack was still in full progress, and not due to finish until half past two in the morning. As James Thompson got into his Jeep, a truck arrived beside him. Out of it came three linemen who had just returned from mending one of the many telephone lines which ran from here towards the front.

"What's the weather like in front?" asked James of one of the party.

---
* Despatch Riders' envelope for messages.

"Not too bad. A few odd shells coming over, but not half as bad as it was last night. Where are you off to, anyway?"

"123 Brigade."

"Look out for the minefield about two miles on this side of them. The wire's been half shot away, and it's darned difficult to see where the minefield begins. Don't say I didn't warn you."

"I'll be careful," said James. In a cloud of dust and sand he drove off in the direction of the flickering horizon.

Almost immediately he had to pass through a long gap in our own minefield. This gap was thick with tanks, ambulances and other vehicles of all sorts and sizes. The ambulances were coming back from the Advanced Dressing Station just at the other side of this gap, in a small wadi which gave it a certain amount of protection from enemy shelling. Not that the fact of its being a Medical Centre would deter the Germans from shelling it, but lying in a wadi, it was difficult for the enemy to get observation on to it, and so it just didn't get shelled at all.

The little Jeep threaded its way through the gap, down into the wadi and up the other side on to 'Moon' track, along which tanks were moving in a very slow procession, each of them about three hundred yards away from the one in front. James carried on along this track for about half a mile, then his way took him off to the left, and he struck out across the desert, following a fairly clearly defined line of empty petrol tins. On the side of each tin was painted the number of the Infantry Brigade he was going out to see.

He smiled to himself as he imagined what would happen if he were to use Desert language when asking a policeman at Home the way. Supposing you were in London and asked the way to Liverpool. Who could imagine the policeman replying: "Follow the petrol tins up Piccadilly till you come to 'Moon' Track. Carry on down there for twenty miles, and then strike off at 137 degrees till you reach the telegraph poles. Follow them for sixty miles, and turn left at Leicester along 'W' Track. That will take you straight into Liverpool. You can't miss it."

How often had James Thompson heard fellows say those fatal words "You can't miss it". As sure as anybody said that, you were bound to get lost and have to retrace your steps to where you had started, and begin all over again.

He had been following the petrol tins for about a mile, then the going began to get very heavy. After several detours, he made the awkward discovery that he had lost sight of the petrol tins, and was right off the track. Still, he had been that direction before, and he really ought not to get lost if he kept on in the same general direction. So, instead of going back along his own tracks, as he should certainly have done if he had had any sense, he stopped and tried to take a bearing from the stars. James fancied himself at the stars, he had been a Boy Scout in the long ago days before he had joined the Army, and he thought that he could recognise a good many of the constellations and individual stars and planets.

What he forgot was that it had been a good time ago when he really did know something about it, and also that he had not paid much attention when his Section Officer had tried to teach him and his brother Don R's on board the ship coming out to the Middle East. So he gaily decided to start off again in the general direction of one star he was quite sure he recognised, and which was what he reckoned to be about vertically above the position of the 123 Infantry Brigade Headquarters.

James, James! After all you had been taught, and you didn't even remember that the stars move!

All went well for about a couple of miles, save that the going became increasingly more difficult. On one occasion he had even to get out and dig one of the wheels free when it stuck firmly in a specially bad piece of deep soft sand. He was still going in approximately the right direction, because he could see the explosions of our own shells on the Australian front, away to his right. But he had not seen any other vehicles or men for quite a long time, and was frankly beginning to feel a little uneasy about having lost his way.

As he was going through a nasty little wadi, a cloud passed across the face of the moon, and the desert became a remarkably dark place after the brilliant moonlight which had favoured his journey so far. He managed to steer the Jeep through the wadi, and up the steep sides at the far end. He stopped for a moment as he came out once again into the open desert, and tried to check his direction. He was sure he was all right, for in the dim distance he could just make out the outline of a piece of rising ground which was very near to the Headquarters of 123 Infantry Brigade. But he was not certain that he had ever approached it from quite this direction. He hoped it would be all right, though he knew full well that there was a pretty wide minefield to cross before he came to the Brigade.

He had to get there somehow, and nothing was to be gained in hesitating. So he set his Jeep in low gear, and started off once more in the direction of that piece of rising ground in the middle distance. All went well for about a quarter of a mile, then, quite without any warning, there was a frightful explosion, and he felt as though a huge hand had taken his Jeep and flung it bodily into the air. There was a blinding flash, and he had the sensation of being flung violently forward. Then he knew nothing more, the world became a blank.

How long he lay there in the sand, he never knew. Gradually he recovered consciousness, and realised what had happened. His Jeep had run into a minefield and one of his wheels had passed over a mine. He lay quite still for some little time, not daring to move for fear that he had collected some dreadful wound. Ultimately, as he did not feel any out of the ordinary pain in his body, he moved his hands and gingerly started to feel himself. First of all his head, that was all right. Then his hands and his body.

They seemed to be quite whole. Then he sat up and took a look at his legs and feet. His right knee was covered with blood, but otherwise all seemed to be well. He investigated his knee, and found that there was a pretty deep gash on the inside of the leg, but he was still able to bend the limb.

With great care, he got unsteadily to his feet and looked around. The Jeep lay on its side about twenty yards away, and the back portion looked rather like a junk-shop for old iron. Both of the wheels had been blown clean off, and the rest of the vehicle lay there twisted and torn so that it certainly wouldn't be any more use to James that night.

He remembered his messages, and looked inside his satchel which he still carried slung around his shoulder. All was well, they were still there, safe and sound.

He tried to walk across to where the Jeep was lying, but no sooner had he taken a step forward than he fell unsteadily to the ground, all in a heap. He was shaking in every limb, and there was a dreadful singing in his head. A moment later he was actually sick.

Afterwards, he lay quite still in the sand, trying to collect enough strength to get to his feet again. The noise of the artillery had stopped, and all over the desert there was silence. He tried to move, but this only made him sick again, so he decided to lie still for some little time, until he felt better.

How long he lay there, he did not know. Perhaps he dozed off to sleep. More likely, it was only a very few minutes. Anyway, after a short time of silence, there came a sudden whistle in the night air, and an enemy shell landed within twenty yards of where he lay. Fear lent him strength, and he got to his feet and started to run. To his eternal credit, he ran in the direction of the 123 Brigade Headquarters, and not back whence he had come. The old devotion to duty of the Despatch Riders of the British Army had come to the fore in his heart, if only subconsciously, and he staggered off through the minefield, in the direction of his goal.

He was aware that at every step he might be blown to little pieces, but he struggled on manfully, conscious only that he had a job to do and that nothing else mattered until that job had been done. Dazed and bleeding, he managed to keep on his feet, and staggered forward through the deep sand.

A kindly Providence saw to it that he did not tread on any mine, and at length he came within sight of the Headquarters of the 123 Infantry Brigade. Some force inside him kept him on his feet till he had found the dug-out where the Brigade Signal Office was sited. Here, unslinging his satchel, he crept in.

"You look a bit washed out," remarked the Brigade Signal Officer as James Thompson entered the confined space where he was working.

James couldn't speak. He merely held out his envelope which the officer took from him. Then a feeling of tremendous weariness overcame him. The world became a dim place, and waves of darkness surged around his eyes and into his brain.

"Sit down, lad," he heard the officer saying, a very long way off. Then he collapsed on the floor of the dug-out.

They covered his body with a blanket, and let him lie in a corner until he felt better. Then they took him off to see a Medical Officer who found that he would be all right after a good rest. So they kept him at Brigade Headquarters till the morning when he went back to Division on a vehicle that was going there anyway. He felt a bit shaky for several days afterwards, and he would never forget that awful journey on foot through the minefield, when he never knew if the next moment would be his last.

His Colonel didn't forget either. It was several weeks later on that James Thompson heard the end of the story. He had been given the Military Medal.

CHAPTER VII

SIGNALS AGAIN

BACK IN HIS LITTLE DUG-OUT, THE SIGNALS COLONEL sat with his Adjutant. There was a telephone on the table between them, and among piles of papers in orderly array stood a thermos flask full of hot tea. The very walls of the dug-out were shaking to the noise of the tremendous barrage which was going on outside. A thin cloud of sand and dust floated down from the roof and settled on everything in the dug-out.

The telephone rang, and the Colonel took up the receiver.

"O.C. Signals here."

A metallic voice answered from the other end.

"Yes, Alec. What is it?"

"The lines to the 234 Brigade are down, Sir. I've sent John's chaps out on it, but we don't know as yet where the break is."

"I see. Well, I expect Spike will have sent out from his end. Let me know as soon as it is through again."

"All right, Sir, I will. One more thing, can you get your hand on another small exchange. It's badly needed here, I understand that several more Gunner Regiments are coming under command pretty soon. I think you'd better get on to the CRA* and find out. Will you do that, Sir?"

---

* Commander Royal Artillery.

"Yes, I'll get a call put through to James at Rear Division and see what he can do about it. If he can produce one, I'll send it up on a truck right away. In fact, I'll probably bring it up myself, as I want to see how your chaps are getting on. I'll do my best, and ring you back soon."

"Sorry, Sir. The GOC* wants me — Good-bye."

"Good-bye."

The Colonel put the telephone down and rang the bell for another call. "Get me Major Greig at Rear Division," he said to the operator, and replaced the instrument.

"You heard all that, Tom ?" he asked the Adjutant.

"Yes, Sir. Didn't Alec say that there would be some additional Artillery Regiments coming under command soon ?"

"Yes. That means I will have to go and see the Brigade Major RA**, and perhaps the CRA as well, if I can manage to get away from here. I'll have James Greig sending up another small switchboard, the ones they have at TAC are pretty full now. They'll never compete with a few more Regiments."

The telephone rang again, and the Colonel answered.

"That you James ?"

"James speaking, Sir," came the reply.

"Look here, ever-faithful, I want another small switchboard for Alec at TAC. Some extra Gunner Regiments are coming under our command soon, and the boards up there are pretty full as it is. What can you do about it ? Have you got any in stock ?"

---

* General Officer Commanding.   ** Royal Artillery.

"Not one, at the moment, Sir. But I'll get on to Graham at Corps and I'll ring you back in a wee while."

"O.K. And if there is any difficulty about it, let me know. I'll have a word with the CSO myself if Graham is sticky. I want to send one up to Alec and his lads to-night. They must get it installed before light or there won't be time left to do it before the Gunners start their next party to-morrow night. So do what you can, my hearty."

"I'll do my best, Sir. And by the way, I managed to get another fifty miles of cable this afternoon. Where do you want it sent."

"Better hang on to it for the meantime, I'll probably want it sent up to Alec's dump at TAC. The Brigades are literally eating the stuff. They seem to think I'm made of cable."

"Well, Sir, I'd better hang up now and get on to Graham."

"O.K. James, good-bye."

"Good-bye, Sir."

The Colonel put down the instrument. "Pour me out a mug of tea, Tom," he said to the Adjutant.

"Certainly, Sir. It's a damned good thing we thought of buying this thermos flask in Cairo. It's coming in jolly handy now."

"You never said a truer word, Tom."

A very tall officer came into the dug-out and saluted the Colonel.

"Hullo, Bill! What brings you here, little stranger?"

"Bad news, as usual, Sir," smiled Wilson.

"Speak up, laddie, I can't hear you for the blasted row your Gunners are kicking up outside."

Captain Wilson was the Signal officer who attended to all the Artillery communications throughout the Division. He usually lived with the CRA and his Staff, and only paid infrequent visits to his own Unit. One of the most popular officers in the whole Division, he was a cheerful young giant who had played several times in the Scottish Rugby Fifteen in the long ago days before the War.

"Eddie Section have had a nasty crack, Sir. They have lost three of their wireless vehicles, complete with sets, during the afternoon Stuka raid. A stick of bombs fell right across the Regimental Headquarters. Mercifully none of the men were hit, but I'm afraid these three vehicles are a complete right-off."

"It never rains but it pours," exclaimed the Colonel. "Have you told James Greig about it?"

"Not yet, Sir. He was out when I rang up, but I left a message for him with the Quartermaster. I don't know how long it will take to get these vehicles and sets replaced. Do you think you can do anything to hurry it along, Sir?"

"I'll do my best, Bill. Hang on a minute while I have a talk to James Greig."

"Hullo, James. Back here again. Did you have any luck with that switchboard? — You did. Good man. When are you sending it up? — Right away. — It's gone already. — Splendid. I'll tell Alec it's on the way. Now I've got a nasty one for you. Bill tells me that Eddie Section have lost three trucks together with the sets in them. — You've heard already. Good. What can you do about it? — Coming up from the Corps park in the morning. — Excellent fellow. I don't know how you manage it all, James my wonderful one. — O.K. I'll tell Bill. I must ring off now. Good-bye."

The Colonel turned again to Captain Wilson.

"You heard that? James says that he can get another three vehicles out of the Corps Park in the morning, and he'll be able to send them up. I suggest you get three drivers from Eddie Section down to TAC after breakfast, to take them over."

"I'll see to that, Sir. Can I use your phone? I'll tell young Oliver they'll be along in the morning, and have him send his chaps to fetch them."

"Go ahead. After that I want to talk to you about these extra Gunner Regiments that I hear are coming under command to-morrow."

"Right you are, Sir."

The Colonel finished his mug of tea and lit a cigarette. Outside, the incessant noise of the barrage went on with monotonous regularity. The walls and roof shook as if they would crumble to pieces at any moment. Occasionally there came a dull thud from not so far away. This would be the explosion of an enemy shell landing in the vicinity of the dug-out. The world had gone crazy. It was a place of fearful noise and fumes of battle. Not far in front of them men were seeking out other men to shoot and to kill. Overhead, there was the incessant drone of aircraft engines and occasionally the scream of falling bombs. The Battle of Alamein was being fought out in all the ghastliness of modern war.

Captain Wilson finished his conversation and turned once more to his Commanding Officer.

"That's all fixed up, Sir," he said. "Oliver will have his men at TAC by nine in the morning. He says they did not manage to save anything from the trucks. They were completely destroyed."

"Bad luck," said the Colonel. "But let's talk about these extra Regiments. Do you know anything about them?"

"Only that there are two Field Regiments and one Medium coming along some time to-morrow, Sir. The CRA doesn't yet know their numbers, but I expect that will have come in when I get back. Are you coming up with me, Sir? I expect you'll want to speak to the CRA, won't you?"

"Yes, Bill, I'll come back with you now. We must find out exactly which these new Regiments are, and just where they are going to. Then you'll have to contact their Signal Officers to arrange lines and give them our wireless dope."

"Will you get John to lay lines to them, Sir?"

"Yes. I'll fix all that once I know exactly where they are to go. I'll try to lay on two lines to each of them, and a few laterals. In fact, as many laterals as I can manage."

"That sounds grand, Sir!"

"Come along then, Bill. I'll take you across to 'A' Mess first, and we'll see if we can get a drink before we go off. Tom, I'm going up to TAC with Bill, and

I don't expect to be back much before three in the morning. You get forty winks now, and young Jimmy can answer the phone. Then you can take over from me when I get back. I'll want a bit of sleep by then, I expect."

"Right you are, Sir. I'll be all right."

The two officers left the dug-out and made their way across in the direction of 'A' Mess in search of a much-needed drink.

Fifteen minutes later they were in the Colonel's Jeep, heading up the line in the direction of TAC Headquarters. There was absolutely nothing on the coast road, as this had been reserved entirely for the use of returning ambulances. The battle had only been started two hours earlier — it was close on midnight — and the first batches of wounded had not begun to arrive from the Advanced Dressing Stations up in the battlefront.

Away to their left, the desert seemed incredibly empty. In the brilliant moonlight they could clearly see the black lines which denoted the newly-made tracks called 'SUN', 'MOON' and 'STAR', along which the tanks would come in about two hours from now. They turned off, down the Quattara Track and headed for the gun positions. The little Jeep found the heavy sand pretty difficult going.

The two officers did not speak as they drove. It would have been little use if they had tried to do so, the artillery was making the night hideous with noise. The barrage was in full swing, it was a most awe-inspiring sound. All around the earth kept being lit up by the brilliant flashes from the hundreds of guns in the vicinity. Both officers had served with the old original Highland Division, the bulk of which was now in captivity after the tragedy of St. Valerie. Both had lost many friends in that bitter fight, and it was a great satisfaction to hear this barrage of hundreds of guns letting fly at the enemy with the enormous weight of modern shells. It was like getting a small bit of their own back. And goodness knows they had had to wait long enough for it.

A mile or so down the track, they met a couple of ambulances driving ever so slowly on their way back to the Main Dressing Station. They were the first of what was later to be a steady stream of vehicles carrying their load of wounded men away from the battlefield and back to the safety and comfort of the hospitals at the Base.

Arriving at the Signal Centre, they walked over to the dug-out where the telephone exchanges were housed. For a moment or two they stood at the bottom of the few steps, waiting for their eyes to get accustomed to the darkness. The dug-out was lit only by one small electric light bulb on the wall, with the leads dangling to a battery on the floor.

Two Signallers were seated at the bank of telephone exchanges, and seemed to be extremely busy. In the far corner of the room, at a small table, sat Captain Alec Foster. He was speaking at a telephone, holding one finger in his free ear to keep out the sound of the guns.

"All right, John," Foster was speaking down the telephone, "tell your chaps to stay out till they get the line through again. It's no use coming back till the job's done. I'll see that a meal is kept for them when they get in. Is that all?" He laid down the instrument and wiped the perspiration from his brow. Then he saw the Colonel and got to his feet.

"Hullo, Sir. Glad to see you, there is a lot on at the moment."

"I've come up to see about these additional Gunners who are coming under command in the very near future," said the Colonel, lighting a cigarette. "Have you heard anything about them?"

"Yes, Sir, I have. The O.C. of one of the Regiments is over with the CRA at this moment. Perhaps you'll go across and see him. I can't get out of them exactly where they intend to go; and I won't ask John to lay any cables until I am quite sure where they go. You know what these Gunners are, Sir. No sooner will I get a line out to them when they'll change their minds and I'll have to lay another to quite a different place."

"Cheer up, Alec," laughed the Colonel. "It won't be as bad as all that. I'll go across to see the CRA and get him to say exactly where these chaps are going to sit down. I can assure you, I won't ask you to lay any lines at all until I am quite clear where they are going. I'll have the Signal Officer of each Regiment clock in with Bill here and stick a flag into the very spot they chose for their Headquarters."

"It's the only way, Sir," agreed Captain Wilson, with a grin. "These Gunners are the most volatile people in the world."

"All right, Alec," went on the Colonel. "Don't you worry your head about it, I'll fix it with the CRA. He's an old Signal Officer himself, you know."

"I know that, Sir. He's grand himself, I agree. But I still won't believe they are going to where they say until I actually see them there. I've been bitten far too often before."

"Here's a bottle of beer to cool off with," laughed the Colonel, producing one out of his haversack.

"Now, Sir, I call that real gentlemanly of you." Alec Foster beamed all over his face with delight. "Are you quite sure you can spare it, Sir?"

"Quite sure, old son. And now we must off to see the CRA. My God! What a row these gunners make with their infernal machines! I hope I won't get so deaf this war that I can't hear the pictures ever again."

"I'm not bothering my head about after the War just now, Sir. I'm only hoping for my lines to stay through for the rest of to-night."

"We'll struggle through somehow, Alec", laughed the Colonel and left the dug-out with Captain Wilson. They walked the four hundred yards through the gap in the mine-field to the small wadi where the General had placed his Battle Headquarters. Here they made their way down into the large dug-out, where the CRA was working next door to the GOC. It was a very small room, and had to accomodate two Signallers and a wireless set as well as the CRA and his Brigade Major. They finished their business as quickly as possible and came out once more into the night air. Just as they emerged from the shelter of the dug-out there was a whine and whistle in the air above them, a little way ahead in the direction of the enemy.

"Down, Bill!" shouted the Colonel, and both officers flung themselves flat in the sand. The whine of the approaching shell lasted really only about three seconds, but to the officers, lying with their heads buried in the ground, it seemed like years till the explosion came. The shell landed about twenty yards from where they lay, and they were covered with sand and small particles of rock thrown up by the blast. For a few moments they continued to lie there, expecting another shell to come over at any moment. But no more came, and they got to their feet.

"Phew! That was a near one, Sir," said Wilson with a short laugh.

"Quite near enough for me, Bill," replied the Colonel. They hurried away to the Signal Centre where they had left their Jeep. They went down into the dug-out to tell Captain Foster what they had arranged with the CRA about the additional Artillery Regiments. It was decided that Captain Wilson would remain forward to see the new Regiments in, while the Colonel went back to Division to see about stores which had to be got forward somehow or other before the next night.

"I'll be off, you chaps," he said. "If I don't go now, I'll never be able to get across the tracks for the tanks. They are due past Alamein Station in half an hour from now.

"Bring me some more beer when next you come up, Sir," grinned Foster.

"Thirsty devil," laughed the Colonel as he got into his Jeep. "I suppose you'd like a case of Glen Grant Whisky as well, wouldn't you?"

"What beautiful thoughts you have, Sir," laughed Alec Foster. Then a Sergeant appeared at the entrance to the dug-out and called his name. "Excuse me, Sir. I'll have to run." With that he disappeared into the Signal Office.

"Cheero, Bill," said the Colonel to Captain Wilson.

"Good luck, Sir. See you in the morning."

"Good night." The Colonel drove off down the track towards Divisional Headquarters. He had made all arrangements for the Artillery Regiments, but there was much to be done when he got back to his office, and he would not be able to sleep for several hours as yet. He would have to wait till the Regiments arrived to assure himself that all was well with them before he could rest with an easy mind. His was a job of absorbing interest, he had hundreds of wireless stations and literally hundreds of miles of telephone cables scattered all over the Divisional front. The responsibility for their success or otherwise was his and his alone.

He was a thoughtful man as he drove slowly back across the desert sands to his office.

CHAPTER VIII

THROUGH AT LAST

THE BATTLE OF ALAMEIN DRAGGED ON AND ON for thirteen weary days. Infantry attacks were made here and there, each one eating a little bit more into the enemy line. Each one meant a few more minefields located and cleared. Each one brought its own quota of German and Italian prisoners, mere boys, for the most part, with a sprinkling of older soldiers who had been in the Foreign Legion and in the ranks of the old Imperial German Army.

Every day all men on that grim battlefield hoped that at long last the Armour would be able to break through, but many were the bitter disappointments which had to be borne, more or less patiently, before that actually happened. It would have been suicidal for the tanks to get through those thickly sown minefields unless the way had been properly prepared by the Infantry and Engineers beforehand. It was a period of wearing down, a gradual crumbling of the enemy's positions. Only first class troops could have stood up to the strain.

One night, a certain Division would be put on to carry out an attack supported by all the available artillery. A good deal of ground would be gained, and the anti-tank mines lifted to make way for the armour which would follow in due course. The next night, another Division would be set a similar task in some other part of the line. And so the crumbling process went on from day to day until the Germans had had enough and started to break away with an eye to retreat.

Young John Gray of the Inverness Regiment lay in his slit-trench and sweated with sheer fatigue. He had hardly slept at all for twelve successive nights and his nerves were feeling the strain. Sixteen out of his original thirty men had been killed or wounded, and he counted himself lucky that it had not been worse. He himself was the only subaltern left unwounded in the rifle companies of his Regiment. They had had fearful casualties in officers. These gallant young men of Scotland had been where you would have expected to find them — right in the front of every attack, leading their men. Three out of the four company pipers had been killed, and two of the company commanders wounded. And yet, the battalion was still in good heart. They had met the enemy on level terms and had beaten him, beaten him hollow. Never once had they failed to make ground when they had attacked, and never once had they failed to repel a counter-attack. — The Highland Division had lived up to its fame.

John heard his company commander approaching. Major Wilson had come through the whole show unscathed. Although he looked very tired and dirty he had lost nothing of his normal good spirits. He sat down beside John and lit a cigarette. It was almost dark, but there was time left to have a smoke in perfect safety.

"How goes it, John?" The question was kindly.

"I'm feeling very tired, Sir, but I'm ready for a good deal yet," said John with a smile. He took out his cigarette case and selected one with deliberate care.

"You and I have got to see this show through, John," went on Major Wilson. "I've no other subalterns left now, so it's up to you and me to keep things going."

"I won't let you down, Sir."

"Of course you won't. I know that. You've been grand, and I can never thank you enough, my lad. It's been a tough time."

"Tougher for Jerry, don't you think, Sir?" remarked John with a wry grin.

"By Gad! That's about the only way to look at it, youngster," answered the Major, drawing hard at his cigarette and blowing the smoke out through his nose in a great cloud.

"What's on to-night, Sir?"

"The usual thing. We are due to attack at ten o'clock. The objective is that bit of high ground about two miles in front of us. Can you see it over there?"

John peered out into the gathering darkness.

"Yes, Sir. I can see what you mean. Are you having a conference later on? I expect you will, won't you?"

"Yes. After the C.O. has given out his orders. I'm going across in a short while to get them. He's away with the Brigadier at the moment, but he'll be back any time now."

"I don't believe the Colonel's slept a wink all the battle, Sir," said John with a little laugh. "I don't know how he keeps going at all."

"He's a marvel, I agree," replied Wilson. "Think of the responsibility he carries on his shoulders. I should hate it."

"When do you think you'll get a battalion, Sir?"

The Major laughed. "You never can tell, my son. Anything might happen now. You might find yourself with a company before you're much older. We've had bad casualties in officers, you know. It'll be hard to replace them."

"And yet, Sir, this is what we have all been training for during the last three years, isn't it?"

"It is, my son. But it is nevertheless a bit hard to see all your friends getting bumped off at this rate, isn't it?"

"I agree, Sir. But you can't stop to count the cost when you go into battle, can you, Sir?"

"No, youngster, you can't. You'd never go into battle if you did."

"Are we getting a barrage to-night?"

"I expect so. We've had one each time so far, and I can't see the Brigadier putting us into a show without a barrage at this stage of the proceedings. So don't go worrying your head about these little details."

"I'm not worrying, Sir. I'm much too tired to do that." John yawned with sheer fatigue.

The Major got to his feet. "Well, John, I'll be off to see what the C.O. has to tell me about to-night's party. You'd better try to get some sleep. I'll come back and tell you all when I know it myself. Cheero!"

"Cheero, Sir."

The Major melted away into the darkness. John lay back in his trench and fell fast asleep.

* * *

The Signals Colonel made his way across to the tin-roofed dug-out which housed 'A' Mess of the Division. He was feeling almighty tired. And well he might, he had had precious little sleep for more than fourteen nights. Into the bargain, he had not had his clothes off for all of that period. Things had gone fairly well in his department, far better than he had ever dreamed that they would. But it had been a great strain. Telephone lines had been continually broken by artillery fire, and by the tracks of tanks and other armoured vehicles. Wireless sets had failed, or had been destroyed by Stuka raids. Both men and sets had had to be found from somewhere to replace them. He had spent his time between visiting every unit in the far flung Division, and his office, near to the Divisional Staff where he could get red-hot information as to how the battle was progressing. Every move meant additional telephone lines to some unit, and more wireless detachments to be moved here and there to meet extra requirements. It was an exacting task, but he enjoyed it. After all, he too had been training for this all his life. The proof of the pudding was coming out in the eating.

He entered the little Mess and found the GSO 1 there.

" 'Evening, Eric," he said, as he sat down. "How's the great Staff?"

"Not too bad, Peter. How's the Master Twiddler?"

"Tired but satisfied," laughed the Colonel. "More than I can ever expect any of my many customers to be."

They both called for a drink and settled down to enjoy their meal. They had hardly started into their soup, when there was a familiar whine in the air above the roof of the Mess, and a sharp crack almost above their heads.

"Blast these Bosche!" exclaimed the G 1. "Why can't they leave a man to eat his dinner in peace?"

They both went on eating their soup as if nothing had happened, and in a few moments another shell exploded a little nearer than the last.

"Unpleasant people, these Germans," remarked Peter, as he sipped a whisky and water. — "There's salt in the water again."

"Now, now. You mustn't grumble. You're darned lucky to have any whisky at all."

"True, oh queen! But I don't like salt in it for all that," grinned Peter, as another shell burst almost outside the doorway, and the Mess staff grovelled on the ground.

A few more shells came across, then they stopped as suddenly as they had begun. Neither Peter nor the G 1 said anything about them, but both had a feeling of relief in their hearts when the awful crashes ceased outside. You don't pay much attention to sudden death when you are facing it every moment of the day, but it is none the less unpleasant to face.

"What's the programme for to-night?" asked Peter at length.

"The Inverness Regiment is doing a show over towards the Daba Track. We think that the Bosche is preparing to withdraw altogether, and they may or may not meet any opposition. It is just possible that the Bosche may have gone when they put in their attack. They are hard at it patrolling just now, but they don't cross the Start Line till ten o'clock. If they have gone, I expect that we'll be on the move ourselves by the morning."

"Where do you think we'll go to?"

"That I can't say, but I should think it would be somewhere in the vicinity of Daba Aerodrome. The Armoured Cars have been directed on that point, and I expect they'll just about get there by daylight, if all goes well."

"In that case, Eric, I think I'll be off to warn my braves. I'd better have Alec and his merry men all tee'd up, ready to start. And I think it would be just as well if I ran on ahead myself to find the next place for Divisional Headquarters. Don't you think so?"

"Yes, I do. But you'd better have a word with the General before you start running off on your own. After all, we haven't made certain that the Bosche have decided to go yet, so don't be in too much of a hurry to run off ahead."

"Don't you worry. I'm no hero."

With that, Peter left the Mess for his office dug-out, to warn Alec Foster and his party to be ready to move any time after midnight.

* * *

But no move was to come for Divisional Headquarters that night. The attack of the Inverness Regiment had to be postponed until dawn, owing to the impossibility of laying on the necessary artillery arrangements in the time available before ten o'clock that night. The infantry was able to put in a good deal of offensive patrolling in front of their sector, and gained much valuable information about the enemy dispositions. If the Germans had made up their minds to withdraw, they certainly kept it a close secret. All through the night, an incessant stream of shells from field guns and 205 millimeter guns came hurtling over on top of the Inverness Regiment, and into the gun positions sited a little way behind them.

In the Dressing Stations, the tireless teams of doctors and surgeons laboured away at their work of mercy. There seemed to be no end to the succession of wounded men who had to be brought back from the scene of the fighting. There were many who never lived to see even the Advanced Dressing Stations, far forward though these were. But the large proportion of the wounded were not too badly hurt, and quite a number were able to walk without assistance. It was as well, for these men would be fit again before very long. A short time spent at a Base Hospital and in a Convalescent Centre, and they would be as right as rain and able to re-join their comrades in the fighting line.

It spoke volumes for the morale of the Eighth Army that in almost every case, when a man was hit, his one worry was that he might not get back to his own unit. As far as was humanly possible, men were sent back to the unit from whence they had come. A man fights all the better for being amongst his friends.

Dawn found Captain Alec Foster dozing inside the Signal Office dug-out. He had been waiting all night for any possible news of an advance. He was a most interested party. He had the task of taking forward certain signal detachments to prepare the new location for the Staff when they decided to move. You can't just lay on a complicated system of field telephones all in the twinkling of an eye. It takes a good deal of forethought and preparation.

There are those who say that warfare is made up of moments of intense fright coming in the middle of long periods of excessive boredom. Captain Alec Foster would have said that it was made up of an eternal, quite unmeasured period of intensive work, punctuated at certain times by moments of tremendous excitement. Of boredom, there was precious little for the likes of him. He hadn't the time to be bored.

As it was getting light, Foster got up from his blankets and made his way across to the hole in the ground which answered to the name of the Signals Officers' Mess. Several officers were already eating their breakfast. He threw his hat on the ground and sat down at the table.

"Waiter! Bring me something to eat."

"Coming, Sir. Won't be a minute."

A few moments later, a soldier servant placed a bowl of hot porridge in front of Foster.

"I wonder if the Bosche gets porridge for his breakfast?" Alec smiled.

"I hope their cooks poison it if they do," chimed in one of the subalterns.

"Judging from the appearance of some of their prisoners I have seen in the last few days, I don't think they get very much to eat at all," said Douglas Macdonald, a tall, weatherbeaten subaltern sitting at the end of the table.

"I must say they looked a poor lot," replied Foster, finishing his porridge. — "What's next? Waiter!"

"Here you are, Sir." The man was standing right behind him, and placed a plate of bacon on the table.

"I really don't know how you fellows manage to get us this food, Baker," said Foster to the servant.

"It's all part of our Austin Reed Service, Sir," grinned the man as he walked away.

Suddenly, from the distance came the sound of shots. These quickly became a fusilade, and the light anti-aircraft guns immediately joined in. The noise was rather like the rivetting shop of some ship-building yard.

"Here we go. The morning party as usual," said Foster, getting to his feet. "Let's find a hole."

All the officers who had been having breakfast got up hastily and scattered in every direction in search of slit-trenches. Nobody expected anyone else to stand on ceremony at these times. You just ran as hard as you could for the nearest shelter, and you well knew that you had only about half a minute to get there before the party started.

It was one of the many Stuka raids. The Germans always seemed to do these things at mealtimes. They usually came over at breakfast, and again at lunchtime. After that, they waited till about last light, just the time when most people were eating their evening meal. It was most annoying, to say the least of it.

Foster hopped into a convenient slit-trench and lay down on his back to watch the proceedings. He couldn't see very well in this position, so he sat up and looked into the sky. The whole heavens appeared to be full of little white puffs, the exploding anti-aircraft shells. But as yet he had not seen any Stukas. Yes, there they were ! Five, seven, eight, eleven — fifteen of them. They were not flying in any formation, but were weaving in and out of the 'Flack', apparently watching for any target that presented itself.

Troops on every side were letting fly with their small arms. You were just as likely to get hit by some enthusiastic youngster who let his bren-gun fall too low, as to be blown to pieces by a bomb dropped from one of the enemy planes. It was all a very trying process.

Foster watched the fifteen planes circling about in the sky directly overhead. They would not drop their loads of bombs unless they got the chance of doing some sort of a dive. Suddenly, the leading Stuka broke away from the others and dived straight at something about a quarter of a mile away. Foster could not see from where he lay what it was, but it would probably be some vehicles which had not been properly dispersed. This was what usually happened when a Stuka started to take an interest.

Alec could hear the horrible high-sounding whine of the plane as it sped towards the earth. Any moment now and it would release its load of bombs. But this was not to be for that particular Stuka. One moment the watching men on the ground saw a diving aeroplane, the next it was just an incandescent mass of fire crashing towards the ground. A lucky A-A shell, or an accurate one, have it which way you like, had hit the aircraft fair and square amidships, and the whole thing had burst into flames in a matter of split seconds.

Down it came, like a ball of fire, and hit the ground with an apalling crash, not very far from the vehicles which it had sought to destroy. The troops round about sent up a rousing cheer, and went on letting fly at the other Stukas with every firearm they possessed.

Three of the remaining planes went into a dive and managed to drop their bombs. Great clouds of smoke immediately rose from the place they had landed, but Alec Foster could not see whether they had hit anything or not. He hated the sickening 'crump' as each bomb exploded. A Stuka raid is a nasty thing, there is absolutely nothing you can do about it, once you have found a slit-trench, unless you happen to have a machine-gun handy.

As he watched the moving planes, Alec suddenly saw them turn away towards the German lines and streak off at the rate of knots. He was at a loss to understand what had happened, when he realised that all the Anti-aircraft had stopped firing as well as the troops round about. He looked in the other direction and his heart gave a bound. There, in the early morning sun, roaring flat out towards the West at about five hundred feet, came a whole squadron of the latest type of Spitfires. Overhead they went, with their pale coloured fusilages glistening in the sun.

What a grand sight it was, thought Alec as he clambered out from his hiding-place. He watched the chase as long as he could see the British planes. But it looked as though those Stukas had made good their escape, there were none left within sight. Later in the day, he heard that the Spitfires had managed to overtake three of them and shoot them down in flames.

The Signal Officers hurried back to their mess to finish their interrupted breakfast.

* * *

The attack of the Inverness Regiment was successful. It could hardly have been otherwise, because, when they neared their objective, it became patently obvious that the enemy had gone. There was no answering fire from the sandy hills ahead, and no shells came over to impede the advancing infantry. All night long, the tanks of the Armoured Divisions had been streaming through, well to the left of John Gray's Company. He could hear the clattering of their tanks, but in the darkness and the clouds of sand he could not see anything of their steel shapes. They sounded very near, but then, tanks always do if they are within a couple of miles.

The waiting infantry heard the sounds of far distant gun-fire, which would be the armoured cars, well ahead of the tanks, creating havoc and confusion behind the enemy lines. The Jocks of the Highland Division felt pleased with themselves. And well they might! They had pounded and pounded at the enemy for thirteen solid days and nights, trying their level best to clear aside the minefields, and to make a way for the tanks to get through and behind the enemy's flanks.

Things were getting to a fluid state, and the Signals Colonel went forward in his Jeep to see what he could find out from the troops up in the front. Somewhere in the maze of sandy tracks he came across his young relative, Walter Mitchell. The boy was bending over a small wireless set, trying to make it work.

"Hullo, youngster!" said the Colonel. "Fancy seeing you here."

"Hullo, Peter!" The boy looked up and smiled. He was appreciably thinner than he had been a couple of weeks before, and had two day's stubble on his chin.

"I can't make this blasted thing work, Peter," he said. "Can you spare the time to have a look at it?"

"Anything to oblige a gentleman," smiled the Colonel, and sat down on the ground to see what he could do.

There wasn't very much wrong, and his practised hand soon found the fault. "Tut tut! After all the trouble I've taken with you, my child."

"Perhaps I'm just too tired to think, Peter."

"Have you had a bad time, old son?"

"Fair to middling. I wish I could get some sleep. Do you think there'll be any chance of getting some soon?"

"You can sleep like a log to-night, Walter, my son. The Bosche has done a bunk all right. You'll get peace for to-night, I can promise you."

"Thank the Lord for that, I'm just about dead beat, Peter." The young officer yawned. "Care for a sip of bubly?"

"What!" Peter almost yelled. "Have you got any?"

"Come along with me." Walter led the way along an ill-defined track to where some Jocks were sitting beside a few bushes. Here he stopped and called to one of the men who was sitting a little way apart from the rest of the group.

"Pearson!"

The man got to his feet and came up.

"Yes, Sir?"

"Bring Colonel Denman a mug of the old and bold, if you've got any left. Have you?"

"Just a wee droppie, Sir. I'll get it if you'll bide a minute." He went back to his clump of bushes and started rummaging in the sand. After a moment or two, he produced a bottle and a couple of mugs and handed them to Walter.

"Here's your very good health, Sir," he said with a broad grin. "It's the real stuff, and no mistake."

"You ought to know, Pearson, you used to sell it before the War, didn't you?" laughed Walter.

"I did that, Sir. And I wish I was still selling it now." The man left them to it, and Walter poured out two mugfulls of the precious liquid. He lifted his mug till it touched Peter's.

"God bless you."

"God bless."

They drank in silence.

Peter broke it first. "Do you remember those Sundays we used to spend at the old Crook Inn on the Moffat road?"

"Do I just! I wish to God we were there now instead of in this rotten desert."

"Cheer up, Walter. Those days will come again before so very long, I feel sure. We'll all drive out again to the Crook Inn and drink gallons and gallons of beer, just like we used to do."

"Don't, Peter, I can't bear it."

"You get down to it and have a decent sleep, old son. You look as if you could do with it."

"Yes, I think I will. What are you going to do? I suppose going back to live in the lap of luxury at Division."

Peter laughed. "Not quite that, laddie. I'm off to have a rekko at the next place we are due to stop at. I expect that will be about Daba, or thereabouts. Now I think of it, I'd better be going. Thank's for the bubly. Where on earth did you get it?"

"One of my Jocks found half a dozen bottles in an Italian dug-out. Clever of him, wasn't it?"

"I hope you let him drink a good deal of it."

"Oh, yes. I only kept one bottle for myself, and you've drunk half of that, you old sinner."

"You're far too young to have a whole bottle of champagne to yourself," laughed Peter. "Well, I must away to my job of work. See you sometime. Take care of yourself."

"Cheero, Sir."

"Bye-bye."

Peter got back into his Jeep and continued on his way. For the rest of that day he was busy finding out what was going to happen in the future, and making arrangements for the advance. Not till it was nearly dark did he run the GOC to earth. The General had been out all day with the Corps Commander. The battle had reached the stage of the Fog of War, and it was very difficult to find out where everybody was, and where the enemy had got to. One thing was clear, the Armour had got clean through and was by now ranging far and wide behind the German lines. Whether they had been in time to cut off their retreat to any appreciable extent remained to be seen. But the static part of the battle of El Alamein was finished. The mobile part was about to begin.

Peter had hardly seen the General when he was told to gather a few of his Signals together and hurry on ahead towards Daba, where he was to look for a good place to put Divisional Headquarters. He immediately warned the Adjutant, and had a party detailed to be ready within half an hour. Then he went over to the lorry in which 'A' Mess travelled, and had a scrap meal.

Half an hour later, his little party was well out on the track heading in the direction of Daba, a small village near the sea. He did not know exactly where the enemy was, but the tanks and armoured cars had got well ahead, so it ought to be all right for his small party of about ten vehicles to proceed along this track.

The going was terrible, and soon it was so dark that it became quite impossible to see the outline of the track. The only thing to do was to drive by the telegraph poles which followed it. After about two hours of this sort of going, the Colonel heard the drone of an aeroplane overhead. Suddenly there came the familiar whistle of a bomb descending. The crash of the explosion and the flash of the burst seemed far too near for their liking, so the little convoy halted and dispersed for a while, to see whether any more bombs were dropped. Two more sticks straddled the track just in front of them. The Colonel decided to dig in where they were for the night, and start off again at first light. Flares were dropping in the distance, away to the South where the other part of the battle was still going on. For all they knew, they might be behind the enemy lines. As a matter of fact, they were, but it wasn't until the next day that they found this out!

Sentries were put out at the four corners of the leaguer, and the little party settled down to make the best of it for the night. Few of them had had much sleep for nearly two weeks, and they slid thankfully between their blankets. Thus, without knowing it, they came to the end of the Battle of El Alamein.

CHAPTER IX

INTERLUDE

For the men of the Highland Division, the battle of Alamein ended very suddenly. One evening they were hard at it carrying out an attack on the German position at Tel el Aqqaquir, and the next morning they found themselves far behind the battle front. The Armoured Forces had at long last burst through the enemy lines, and were creating havoc and destruction far and wide along his lines of communication.

After one day spent in making the arrangements, the whole Division was concentrated between Daba and Fuka, along the coast of the Mediterranean. There was a good deal of mopping-up to be done. The enemy had left behind many small parties which had been cut off from their comrades in the mad rush to get away from the advancing Allied Army. Day after day, constant streams of prisoners came marching back, each with its little escort of Jocks. But, for the most part, there was little else to be done but reorganise and let the men have the opportunity of getting a bathe in the cooling waters of the sea.

All along the shore, each day, there could be seen small parties of men swimming about, naked as they were born, happy as sand-boys. Few of them had had any chance of even a decent wash for many weeks past, and it was a real joy to take off clothes which were more than a little dirty, and splash about in the warm salt water of the sea.

There are few greater pleasures in life than just being able to have a bathe, to wear clean clothes and to eat good food, if you have had to go without all of these for a very long time. The men of the Eighth Army had had a bad time. They had lived and fought in the grimy sands of the desert, and their bodies had become caked with dirt. Little wonder that they revelled in the chance of a bathe in the sea.

The Inverness Regiment had been allotted a camping site in a rather picturesque small wadi at the top of some high cliffs which overlooked the sea. John Gray nosed around and discovered a lavish-looking Italian dug-out which he persuaded young Walter Mitchell to share with him. There was ample room for both their camp beds, and what was more, they were able to stand up without bumping their heads against the corrugated iron roof.

Late in the first afternoon, both youngsters were to be found divesting themselves of most of their equipment preparatory to stealing an hour's sleep on their beds before tea. Young Mitchell was bending down to unfasten his boots, while John Gray was stretched out on his bed, smoking a cigarette of Italian origin.

"Thank God for the chance of a rest, Walter," said John, exhaling luxuriously a dense cloud of tobacco smoke.

"How long do you think we'll stay here?" asked Walter, throwing his boots into a corner with a flourish.

"Can't say. But it can't be too long for me. I'm tired of battle for the moment."

"So am I. Every time the C.O. can't speak to one of the Companies on the wireless he blames me for the beastly things not working. And it's usually because he isn't doing the right thing with his handset. I get so tired of being blamed for everything that goes wrong."

"Poor old Signals, nobody loves you, eh, Walter?"

"It's all very well for you to speak. You lie in a slit trench and hog it for hours, while I have to spend my time crawling on my stomach along every cable that gets cut. *And* I don't ever get any thanks for it either."

"Poor old Walter. It isn't as bad as all that, now is it?"

"I don't suppose it is, John, but my wretched Signallers always seem to get the blame for everything that doesn't go right. I'm a bit fed up with it all. I think I'll ask to be sent back to the Rifle Companies before long."

"No, come on, old boy. You'd better not do that. You have done jolly well so far, and I'm sure that the Colonel wouldn't have you changed for anything. I heard him say only the other day that he was lucky to have you as his Battalion Signal Officer. You are appreciated, even if you do collect a few rockets occasionally. You want a spot of leave, that's all that's wrong with you."

"Leave! I wish to goodness I could get some leave. When did you last get any, John?"

"In March last. I got seven days embarkation leave in Scotland before we sailed. I haven't had a day since then, and I don't see us getting any more for the devil of a long time. It looks as if we had to chase the Bosche as far as Benghazi after all. What a life!"

"What are you going to do after the War, John?"

"Do? I don't know. Perhaps I'll ask to stop on in the Army, if they'll have me."

"I want to stay on and be a Regular Officer, but I shall insist on having a month's leave first, you bet your boots about that."

"My dear chap! There won't be any leave for any of us after we've beaten the Bosche. We'll all have to go off and fight Japan. Don't be silly and talk about leave. There won't be any, that's all."

"Perhaps you're right, but surely somebody will have to police the occupied countries after we've knocked out Germany? We can't very well leave Germany to the tender mercies of the Poles and the Czechs and the French and the Danes, and all the people who have been conquered. They'd murder all the Germans till there wasn't anyone left."

"Well, why not?"

"You can't destroy a nation, or at least they say you can't."

"Why not? I'll bet the Germans would have a darned good shot at destroying us if they beat us, don't you think so?"

"I expect you're right. But the innocent Germans would suffer as well as the guilty."

"I don't believe there are any innocent Germans. They're all the same, or you wouldn't get the thousands of Gestapo and hired thugs in their various uniforms all ready to beat up old women and young children. They must all of them be a pretty beastly race, and after all, they've upset the peace of the world five times in the last hundred years. Why on earth should they ever be allowed to do it again?"

"If we were to educate them properly, that should do the trick."

"Why bother? Why not destroy the lot of them and let the world have a chance to live in peace for a while? I don't believe in being kind to the Germans after this war. Kill the lot, that's what I say. You'll never get peace as long as there's a German left. They've forfeited the right to world citizenship. It's they who started the mass bombing of large cities. Put them down, they're just a disease, that's what they are, a disease."

"Perhaps you're right, John. In any case, I want to go on leave. I look forward to the day when I can be driving out of London in a new car, with a couple of suitcases in the back, and my golf clubs and a fishing rod. I'd just go wherever I felt like for a whole month. That's what I want to do after the war, don't you?"

"You bet I do, but I'm afraid that I'm more likely to have to leap on to a ship and go off to fight those wretched little Japs."

"Ah well, what's the use. I'm going to get some sleep. It's not much good trying to put the world right before we've cleaned up this little lot." Walter yawned and lay back on his bed. In a few minutes, both subalterns were sound asleep.

* * *

Colonel Forsyth was sitting alone in the Mess tent with Major Wilson, the commander of 'A' Company of the Inverness Regiment. They had come in late for tea, and were the only officers left in the tent. The Colonel had been for a bathe in the sea. The Major had not yet had time to do the same, and looked as dirty and tired as his Colonel looked clean and refreshed.

"What was your total number of casualties, Bill?" asked the Colonel at length.

"Fifteen killed and thirty nine wounded, Sir. It might have been worse. And some of the wounded ought to be able to get back again before very long."

"It's not half as bad as it would have been in a similar battle in the last war," mused the Colonel as he sipped his tea out of a huge tin mug. "I can well remember our companies going into a show at nearly full strength, and coming out with only two men and a boy left. It hasn't been anything like that this time, thank the Lord!"

"I think that is because our lads are learning the value of keeping well dispersed, don't you think so?"

"There's a lot in that. As long as they don't crowd together there's a good chance of getting away with it. And, as you say, they're learning."

"It's a pity we lost so heavily in officers. These youngsters are made of good stuff. Young Gray of mine put up a grand show."

"You mustn't forget to put his name in for an award, Bill. I'll be calling for names to-morrow. I want to do that while we remember all about it. It's far better to stick these things down on paper while the memory is trustworthy, otherwise the show goes on and more things happen to make us forget the bravery of yesterday."

"I'll think up a few names, Sir."

The Colonel poured himself out another mug of tea and lit a cigarette. Then he sat back in his chair and puffed the smoke out in great clouds.

"Young Walter Mitchell did awfully well, Bill," he went on. "That lad had a sticky job, and I was chasing him all the time. I know he thinks I don't give a tinker's damn for him and his precious band of Signallers. But he's wrong. I think very highly of him indeed, they did a very fine job of work. I'm going to put him in for an M.C. when the periodical awards come along. I can't very well put him up for an Immediate, he didn't do any one conspicuously gallant act. He just carried on throughout the whole battle. And they don't give Immediate Awards for that, the more's the pity. It's a funny thing, that, Bill. The chap who rushes into action and saves the Colonel's life gets a V.C. But the bloke who just carries on with his job for days and weeks, perhaps without any sleep to speak of, he can't get anything at all, unless he is very lucky indeed and collects a 'Ration gong' later on."

"Ah well! Sir. You wouldn't like to see medals and decorations thrown about too much, would you? It would cheapen them, wouldn't it?"

"I quite agree, Bill. After all, what's in a little bit of ribbon? It's the beating of the Bosche that really counts. Still, I'd dearly like to get you all the V.C. You richly deserve it!"

They both laughed, but Major Wilson knew what the Colonel meant. He was voicing in some little measure his abounding pride of his Battalion. Just then the Adjutant came into the Mess tent with a piece of paper in his hand.

"Hullo, Dickie!" remarked the Colonel. "You look like business. What's it all about?"

"We're off again, Sir. There's a conference up at Brigade for you at seven o'clock. Evidently they've spotted some enemy from the air, and Brigade are sending out a column to round them up."

"Where are these enemy?"

"About twenty miles South from here, Sir. But there aren't many details. I only gathered from the Brigade Major that we and some artillery are to be ready to move at first light."

"Have you warned the Company Commanders?"

"All except Major Wilson here."

"Well done, good and faithful one. Sit down and have a mug of tea."

"I've had mine, thank you, Sir. I think I'll be getting back to the office. There's a big return due to go off to the Base in the morning."

"This war will just *have* to end before very long, Dickie," laughed the Colonel. "The world will run short of paper, and then it'll have to stop."

"It can't stop soon enough for me," grinned Major Wilson.

"I must be getting back, Sir," said the Adjutant, "are you coming over soon?"

"I'll be across in a few moments. Just let me finish my mug of tea and I'll be after you."

The Adjutant left the two senior officers, and went off in the direction of the Battalion Orderly Room. He was a great man for work, and rarely came out of his office when the battalion was at a standstill.

"I wonder what this all means, Bill?" said the Colonel.

"Some stray Bosche getting above themselves, Sir, I expect. It might be fun rounding them up."

"I'd rather stay here and let the men get a bit of a breather. They could do with a rest and a bathe in the sea."

"I shouldn't think it means a long job, Sir. It may take us about a couple of days, and after that we'll get back here in time for a few days' easy for the men."

"You're probably right, Bill. The Armoured Boys must be getting a long way ahead now. We'll have to be moving off after them before very long. But there's bound to be a bit of mopping-up to be done every time we stop like this."

"Bound to be, Sir. But I wish we could be getting on, all the same. We'll never win the war by sitting

General inspection. Montgomery greets the author on his arrival at 51 Div. Signals HQ.

The author presents his second in command to General Montgomery.

Monty shares a joke with the author's R.S.M.

51st Div. Signals HQ at El Agheila when inspected by Gen. Montgomery in December 1942.

O.C. Signals office at TAC HQ 51 Div. during the battle of Alamein, picture taken in November 1943.

Alamein Station, November 1943.

The "Bombay Road", November 1943.

G OPS office 51 Div. at Alam el Halfa, after one year, November 1943.

back here, while the Germans make good their retreat."

"I don't think you need worry about that, Bill. The Army Commander isn't the man to let them alone, even for a day or two. He'll have us off and after them just as soon as he can. It's probably all a matter of supplies. You can't move a huge army like ours across hundreds of miles of desert without pretty adequate administrative arrangements. There must be thousands of gallons of petrol and water to be got forward before all those tanks and lorries can move a yard. And the food, it's a perpetual marvel to me how we always seem to be able to get our rations, whether we are in the middle of a battle or not. There's a devil of a lot of quartermongering work to be done before you can send an army helter skelter after the Bosche for an indefinite distance. You can't move a yard without planning your supplies ahead."

"You're right, Sir. These 'Q' chaps are a ruddy marvel. It amazes me how they manage to do it all. Thank the Lord I failed to pass into the Staff College before the War. If I hadn't failed, I might well have been a 'Q' Staff Officer by now."

"That being so, we wouldn't have any food or petrol at all, eh Bill?"

They laughed. Bill Wilson was a grand regimental officer, but even his best friends agreed that he wouldn't make a very good Staff Officer. He had always been too occupied with games to pay much heed to his books.

"Well, I suppose I'd better toddle off to the office and ring up Brigade to find out what it is all about," said the Colonel, rising from his chair.

"I'll take a look at the troops, I think, Sir," said Wilson, reaching for his bonnet.

They parted at the doorway of the Mess tent and went their separate ways.

* * *

The Signals of the Division had sited their officers' Mess right at the edge of the tall cliffs overlooking the sea. The Mess was a largish tent set up close to the lorry which carried the cooks and stores required to feed the many officers. Inside was one long table, composed of several smaller ones, set side by side. Round this table were about fourteen folding chairs. In one corner, standing on a large packing case, was a wireless set, used chiefly for the B.B.C. News, but usually left switched on whenever there was an officer in the Mess tent. In another corner stood a wooden box containing an assortment of papers and periodicals, all dated several weeks and months previously.

The whole place had the atmosphere of a very temporary and mobile nature, but it was the only place which any of the officers could call 'Home' in this Outpost of Empire tucked away in the Western Desert. It was a very happy Mess, as there was never any fuss and worry about Ranks. Most of the officers had been great friends away back in the days of peace, when they had all belonged to the same Territorial Unit. When the war came, they merely put on uniform, and started to live together each day and every day, instead of meeting pretty well every evening of the week. It was a place where christian names were almost invariably used, except by those who were either very junior, or had only recently joined the unit.

The Mess had gained a very good name for entertaining, and some of their Guest Nights had become famous throughout the Division. But entertaining wasn't quite so easy in the Desert as it had been at home. Water and food were both strictly rationed, and it wasn't at all easy to scrape enough together to feed the extra mouths which continually kept dropping in, especially as they almost always coincided with some mealtime. But, somehow or other, there always appeared to be enough and to spare. The old Quartermaster saw to that.

It was getting dark, and little fires had started up all over the large encamping area, known to the men of the Eighth Army as a 'Leaguer'. The men always fed in little groups. Never was a large body gathered together. This would have provided a heaven-sent target for any roving enemy fighter plane, and there was never enough time for a gathering to disperse before they got shot up. At the top of the highest place in the area, above the Signals Mess, there stood an anti-aircraft gun, the team keeping a constant lookout during the hours of daylight.

Vehicles were scattered widely around the area, no one lorry being closer than a couple of hundred yards from the next, so that an unlucky bomb wouldn't knock out more than one vehicle at a time. This had been amply proved in the late battle, when on one occasion only an enemy Stuka raid had managed to set alight four vehicles at once.

The men were gathering in their washing which had been lying out in the sun since the morning. This had been the first opportunity for getting their clothes washed since the battle had started. Both officers and men were revelling in the comparative amenities of the place, and, in fact, it was a veritable paradise after the heat and the dust of the bullet-swept desert.

The Signals Colonel looked in at his own Mess on his way across to dine with the Divisional Staff. He had his meals with what was called 'A' Mess. Here he lived with the Commander and his principal Staff Officers, and thus was able to be in on any plots which were hatching. Whatever may be said against it, it is a proven fact that officers only get the best out of each other when they live in the same Mess; officers, that is, who work in the closest contact.

Colonel Denman entered the tent and found most of the others already started at their evening meal. Although he did not feed here, there was always a place laid for him, and he invariably took a cup of tea when he stayed to chat with his own officers.

There was a chorus of "Good-evening, Sir" as he sat down in his accustomed place at the table, beside Major Carter, the Second-in-command.

"Good-evening, James," said the Colonel, taking off his hat and throwing it into a corner. "I suppose you are all feeling nice and clean, for a change?"

"Clean and in our right mind," laughed Major Carter. "Baker! Bring the C.O. a cup of tea!"

"Coming, Sir."

"How's your sand-pit, Alec?" asked Douglas Macdonald, one of the subalterns.

"I'm not making any sand-pits out here," grinned Alec Foster.

"I thought you were going to start a Desert Salvage Company after the War," said the Quartermaster with a wink at the Colonel.

"You and your Desert Salvage Companies," retorted Foster. "You might as well make a good start yourself with your rotten old stores."

"I'll take you into partnership, Alec," smiled the Quartermaster.

"No fear 'Q', I'm off back to my own business as soon as this war is finished. No Desert Salvage Companies for yours truly."

"What are you going to do when the war's over, Sir," the Quartermaster asked the Colonel.

"What am I going to do when the war's over? Soldier on, I expect. Don't forget there will be another long war with Japan once we've cleaned up Germany. I only hope I shall be wanted for the Occupied Countries. I have no wish to go off immediately this show is over and swelter in a Malayan jungle, chasing those wretched little men. I don't think it would be any fun fighting the Japs."

"Somebody's got to do it," chimed in Major Carter.

"I quite agree, but all I can say is that I hope it won't be us."

"Don't you think, Sir," said Foster, "that it would

be a good idea after Germany is finished, if they drafted out to fight Japan all the chaps who have stopped at Home so far?"

"Not a bad idea, Alec. But I doubt it won't work out quite like that. However, once Germany is finished, we'll be able to concentrate all our united fleets and air forces on to the Japs. I don't think it ought to take us so very long to settle their hash. All the same, old boy, you won't be seeing your old Kirkcauldy for years and years. You'll be a General before you ever get back there."

"I'm sure I don't want to be a ruddy General. I want to get back to my business. The darned thing must be about broke by now."

"I know what I'll do after the war, James," said the Colonel to Major Carter. "I'll come and be your Adjutant. After all, you're a substantive T.A. Major, and I'm only a poor Captain till January of next year. Don't you think I'd make you a pretty decent Adjutant?"

"Grand, Sir. Then you will be able to do all the work while I get down to golf in a big way."

They all laughed.

"Two minutes to go before the news," said the Quartermaster. "Baker, switch on the News." The Mess waiter bent down and tuned in the wireless set.

"I'll just wait for the summary," said the Colonel, "and then I'll be off to my own dinner. The sight of all this food makes me slightly faint."

"Don't they feed you in 'A' Mess, Sir?" chaffed Alec Foster.

"Now and then. It all depends on how many visitors have dropped in."

"Yes, I suppose you have a good deal of entertaining to do, now and then. Thank the Lord we get decent food here, I've lost enough weight already."

"You always were a little on the fat side, Alec," laughed the Colonel.

The News started and the conversation died down. It was the best part of the day, and the only contact they had with the outside world. The Colonel stayed to hear the summary, then he slipped out to get his own dinner.

* * *

Peter Denman bent down beneath the blankets and entered 'A' Mess. The blankets had been hung over the entrance by way of blackout, with the result that the interior of the Mess always got hot and stuffy after the inmates had been sitting there for any length of time. The place was constructed of sandbags, and over the top had been erected a few semi-circular sheets of corrugated iron. The result was something in the nature of an 'elephant house'. But it gave protection from the elements, and what was more, from anything other than a direct hit from a shell or bomb.

The Mess was empty. The blankets parted and Corporal Clay, the Mess factotum appeared in the entrance.

"Good-evening, Sir."

"Good-evening, Clay. What's for dinner to-night?"

"The usual, Sir. Baked bully and tinned potatoes. After that, I've got a couple of tins of pears. Also, there's a little cheese left over from last night."

"That doesn't sound too bad. Bring me a drink, will you please."

"What would you like, Sir?"

"What have you got?"

"Whisky? Gin and lime? Sherry? That's all there is."

"I'll have a glass of sherry, thanks."

The Corporal went to the drinks-chest in the corner of the little dug-out and produced the sherry. Having set it down, he remained in the room talking to Peter Denman. He always remained near at hand when there was only one officer in the Mess. He liked company and had little other chance of having any gossip.

"When are we likely to be moving on, Sir?" he asked.

"I wish I knew. But it can't be very long now."

"We won't ever win the war by sitting down about these places, will we, Sir? I mean to say, the sooner we get off after the Bosche the better for us all."

"I quite agree, Clay. But you can't throw an army about just as you please. We've got to build up our dumps of petrol and food before we can get on with the job. We'll be off again as soon as they are ready for us, never fear. By the way, how's your wife?"

"Thank you, Sir. She's had a nasty go of 'flu', and was in her bed for a couple of weeks. But she's all right now, though I think she's had a nasty turn."

"I'm so sorry to hear that, but I'm glad she's better again."

The curtains parted and the ADMS came in, followed by the G1 and the CRA. They all sat down and ordered drinks, while continuing with the usual daily gossip which went on in every Mess of the army at this time of day. A few minutes later, the General came in and sat down at his usual place at the top of the table.

"Let's start dinner," he said, rubbing his hands together. "I'm hungry. Corporal Clay! We'll start now."

"Very good, Sir."

"Any news yet of a move, Sir?" asked the ADMS.

"None yet, I'm afraid," replied the General. "But I don't expect we shall be kept here kicking our heels for very much longer now. I'm going to Corps tomorrow and perhaps I'll have some news after I get back."

"What time are you going there, Sir?" asked the G 1, with an eye to his master's affairs.

"Immediately after breakfast, Eric, but I'll be back before lunch."

"I'll tell Arthur to have the car ready for you, Sir."

The General turned to Peter. "Your telephones were working quite well to-day, Peter," he said with a smile. "I had a long conversation with the Army Commander, and he must be well over two hundred miles away. If things go on as well as this, I might perhaps give you a few days' leave in Alexandria."

"That's decent of you, Sir," laughed Peter. "The only thanks poor old Signals usually get is a slight, a very slight, diminution of abuse."

The Mess roared with laughter. They were always pulling Peter's leg about his Signals, and it was just as well that he wasn't too sensitive about it.

"You know, Peter," went on the General. "You Signals chaps must get necks of cast iron, with all the complaints and howls that inconsiderate people throw at you."

"We do, Sir," replied Peter with a smile. "Few people ever stop to consider that we handle many thousands of messages every day, and the percentage of mistakes is very small indeed, in fact it is somewhere in the region of .01 per cent. And yet, when anything does happen to go wrong, they immediately forget all that and start to blame us as being pretty useless chaps. Still, we don't worry. But I sometimes feel like the biblical johnnie who had a hundred sheep and one of them went astray. So he left the ninety and nine and went off to look for the missing one. And when he found it, there was more rejoicing over that one than of the ninety and nine who went not astray."

"I agree with you, Peter," chimed in the G 1. When Signals do make a mistake it is usually a bad one, and it involves so many others. You chaps work continually in the limelight."

"I should have said," put in the CRA, "that 'Evil communications corrupt good manners'."

There was general laughter, and the subject changed to a more or less intimate discussion about officers in the Division and their families at home. These evenings spent in the best of good company, were one of the saving graces of life in the Western Desert. Most days, the officers in the various messes sat on for a couple of hours after dinner was over, discussing all the topics under the sun. There were no cinemas to go to, and no shops to be visited. There were no clubs and no friendly houses where one could spent a pleasant evening with hospitable civilians. So they were thrown back on their own company, and jolly good company it was. One came to look forward to these evenings after a strenuous day in the open air. A good yarn and a merry laugh did much to ease the deadly monotony of life in those sandy wastes of the Libyan Desert.

Peter left the Mess early that night. He was feeling more tired than usual. On his way back to the hole in the ground where he slept, he stopped and looked up at the stars which shone so brilliantly overhead. Away to the North, the Plough stood out from the others, and Peter could see the Pole Star high in the heavens over his native Scotland. He sighed a little sigh of sheer weariness, the weariness of the exile. Did the river still run sweetly underneath the bridge at Ballater ? How long would it be before he had the chance of seeing it again ? How long indeed ? Who could tell ? He shrugged his shoulders and went on to the little dug-out he called his home.

CHAPTER X

FIVE DAYS' LEAVE

MAJOR BILL WILSON, COMMANDER OF 'A' COMPANY of the Inverness Regiment, was worried. His eyes were giving him a lot of trouble, and he was in considerable pain. He wore spectacles as a matter of course, and had done so even since his early childhood, but there had not been anything radically wrong with his sight. It was hereditary astigmatism, worsened by a squint. The violent glare of the tropical sun on the Desert sands had not helped matters. Besides, he had much reading of orders and routine papers to go through, all in small holes in the ground, with very poor light to see by. On top of all this, he had been caught in a bad dive-bombing raid early in the battle, and one of the bombs had dropped so near to him that his face had suffered damage from the blast. The result was that he could not now make any decent use of his left eye, and was getting very worried indeed about it. He suffered constant headaches, and was afraid that the doctors would hear about it, and possibly have him sent back to the Base.

He was a Regular Soldier, and feared that a permanent damage to his eyesight might well mean that his days in the Army were numbered. On the whole, he was a very worried man.

He made up his mind to stick it out as long as he could, and by the time that the Regiment moved on from Daba, he had still not mentioned the subject to the Regimental M.O. But the time would soon come when he would have to take medical advice. These splitting headaches were preventing him from giving his full attention to his job of looking after his Company. Sooner or later he would have to tell the M.O.

The Regiment moved on in easy stages by road. They passed through Mersa Matrouh and Sidi Barrani, bivouaced a night on the road outside Sollum, and then on again in the morning as far as El Adem, South of Tobruk. Here there was a pause of three days, and some of the officers managed to get a run into the town to have a look round. There was a wonderful view from the road, as you approached the town from the East. You came over the brow of a hill and started to descend towards the sea. From the top of this hill you looked across the little land-locked harbour at battle-scarred Tobruk. On the morning that Bill Wilson went in, there was a large hospital ship in the harbour, together with a couple of destroyers. Several other vessels were there, but most of them either sunk, or so badly damaged that they were no good to anybody except for salvage. The houses had been battered about for months, and looked it too. Those of them which still stood, had neither windows nor any doors to speak of. Many of them had no roofs. But Bill Wilson was surprised to see so many buildings occupied after all the tales which had been put out about the bombarding of Tobruk. Most of the houses were in use as offices or stores, but no shops or hotels open where you might have been able to buy a drink. Of civilians there were none.

Tobruk looked for all the world like one of those pictures of scarred French towns in the middle of the last War. The gaiety and laughter had gone out from them. They were mere ghosts of their former selves, and were left to provide a modicum of shelter for such military institutions as were necessary to run the port.

After three days at El Adem, the Regiment got on the move once more and drove westwards towards Derna and Benghazi. They spent two days crossing the green belt which covers the Northern uplands of Cyrenaica, stopping one night at Martuba and the next at a little place called Maraua, some sixty miles North East of Benghazi.

These uplands were a glorious change after the never-ending sands of the Western Desert, not at all unlike the rolling moors of the Scottish Borderland. For miles, green rolling plains stretched away into the distance, as far as the eye could see. Every now and then were small white Italian farms, set up by Mussolini in an effort to colonise the country. These little farm-houses looked quite attractive, but the soldiers had been warned not to enter them at any price, as many of them had been mined, and contained all sorts of booby-traps.

Of booby-traps, there seemed to be no end. In one house, a device had been affixed to one of the keys of a piano so that when this particular key was struck, a current would flow in an electric circuit and a mine would go off, blowing up the entire house with its occupants. In another house, a booby-trap had been cunningly set in the bathroom. By a mechanical device, a mine was to be set off by the thirty second pull at the lavatory chain. The previous thirty one customers would get away with it, but the thirty-second would not live to tell the tale. Many indeed were the instances of Man's Inhumanity to Man!

The Regiment paused for two days in a delightful place near the sea, just to the South of Benghazi. Here the men had an opportunity to bathe and to wash their clothes after their long journey. But their stay here was for two days only, after which they were off once more in a Southerly direction, through Ghemmines and Magrun, to a position slightly North of Agedabia, East of the main road, and hidden away in rather pleasant sand-hills, all covered with grass.

There was another pause here, for a whole week this time, while the Armour ahead disposed of some German opposition. It was obvious that the enemy were withdrawing as slowly as possible to prepared positions of great strength in the area of Mersa Brega and Agheila. A week later, the Inverness Regiment moved forward.

But before they moved on, Bill Wilson and his Colonel had one of the narrowest squeaks of their lives. They had both been having tea in the Officers' Mess, and were walking slowly across the grass to the Battalion Orderly Room. Their Unit had been allotted a large hollow in the sand-hills, and at one end of this was the Colonel's Office, while at· the other was the

Officers' Mess. The men were scattered round the sides of the bowl, but in the middle there was nothing at all.

Bill Wilson and the C.O. had just about reached the middle of this empty part, when Wilson heard the familiar drone of an aeroplane engine behind one of the hills. Immediately afterwards, there came the unpleasant sound of machine-gun fire. It was an enemy Tip-and-Run raid, and when these came along, you didn't wait to ask anybody, you just ran for the nearest slit-trench. If there weren't any slit-trenches, you looked for the nearest hollow in the ground.

Bill Wilson glanced quickly about him, but there were no friendly hollows in this piece of ground. All was as flat as the proverbial pancake. The nearest trenches were at the other end, near the offices.

"Run, Bill!" shouted the Colonel, starting to run himself.

"Blowed if I'll run!" retorted Bill, continuing his stately walk.

But he turned round and saw an enemy fighter plane coming straight for the place where he stood. It was not more than half a mile away, firing little bursts from its machine-guns. Altogether a most unpleasant sight.

Bill Wilson took one look at this plane, and decided that now was the time to remove himself from the line of its flight, or else he would stand an excellent chance of being riddled with machine-gun bullets. So he stood on no ceremony, but bolted like a hare at right-angles to the direction in which the approaching plane was heading. He was not a moment too soon. As he flung himself down on the ground, he saw the sand rising up in little spurts only ten yards from his feet. The bullets were ripping their way along past the place where he was lying.

The noise was terrific, every soldier in the area who could lay his hand on a weapon was firing it at the intruder, and a light anti-aircraft detachment on one of the neighbouring hills was letting off into the bargain.

But the shooting died down as rapidly as it had started, and the German swept on untouched to disappear over the hills into the North, and out over the sea. Bill Wilson rose to his feet and dusted the sand off his clothes.

"Phew!" he exclaimed, "that was a near thing. Are you all right, Sir?"

"Perfectly all right, old boy. But next time I tell you to run, don't wait to let the grass grow."

"I won't."

They continued on their way towards the office. Arrived there they found the Adjutant trying to get a heap of sand and dirt out of his hair.

"What have you been up to, Dickie?" laughed the Colonel.

"I've been grovelling in a slit-trench, Sir," replied the Adjutant, with a broad grin. "Unpleasant people these Germans, aren't they?"

"I'll say they are, my lad. That one very nearly arranged some rapid promotion in this Regiment. He almost got Bill Wilson and me just now. Thank the Lord, I can still run pretty fast!"

Nobody had been hurt by the machine-guns of the intruding aircraft, so the incident passed off as an amusing one, but these straffing attacks did not always prove so unsuccessful. There was one a little later on in which the total bag was three officers, fifteen men and four vehicles. You never could tell.

Four days later the Regiment moved on to a position some ten miles East of Mersa Brega. There would obviously be a considerable period of preparation before a big, concentrated attack could be made upon the enemy's undoubtedly strong position. It would be at least ten days before anything happened, so Bill Wilson approached the Battalion M.O. for advice about his eyes. The Doctor was a good eye man, and prescribed that the trouble could in all probability be put right if Wilson could manage to get a fresh pair of lenses. But the problem was where to find these in the Desert. The Colonel mentioned the matter to the ADMS at Division, and the upshot was an arrangement by which Major Wilson was to be sent back to Benghazi by car where he would catch a plane for Cairo. He could get there in a day, and it would only take three days or so to obtain new lenses, so he ought to be able to get back within five days, and this would be in ample time for the impending battle of Mersa Brega.

Bill Wilson received the news of his journey to Cairo with somewhat mixed feelings. He had never yet been up in the air, and wasn't even now particularly anxious to do so. However, being more or less ordered to go, he made up his mind to enjoy the trip.

He had never been sea-sick, and had travelled once to India and once to West Africa ; and had made the long trip out to the Middle East with the Regiment late that summer. He felt quite confident that his stomach would stand up to an aeroplane. Nevertheless, it was a bit of an adventure to travel for six hours in an aeroplane for the very first time.

He set out early the next day in the Colonel's car. It was close on a hundred miles to Benghazi. The road was filled with a constant stream of heavy lorries and Tank Transporters and the going was very slow. They arrived at Benghazi late in the afternoon. There was just time to see the Air Transport people about his passage on the morrow, and find out where he was to report, before it got dark. He had a friend at Army Headquarters located a few miles away from the airport, and had arranged to stay there for the night.

Next day, after a decent breakfast, he gathered his belongings together and drove down to the aerodrome. Benina Airport was a lovely sight. It lay in a pleasant valley at the bottom of the foothills of Northern Cyrenaica. There was plenty of green grass all around, and Bill found it a sight for sore eyes after the soul-destroying monotony of the Desert. There were tall trees near the hangars, and a few houses in the neighbourhood appeared to have quite reasonable, if neglected gardens. He could well picture the place as a busy civil airport in the days of peace.

Many aircraft of varying types were standing about all over the aerodrome. Most of them were transport planes, but there were also a goodly number of fighters, ready to take off should the enemy decide to pay the place a visit. The hangars bore the marks of recent bombing; we had paid fairly close attention to Benina before it had fallen into our hands. There were still a few damaged German and Italian machines lying about, but they had all been cleared away to one side.

Bill wandered around, inspecting the various types of aircraft, till the Cairo plane came in to land. It was a Lockheed Hudson monoplane, and looked very nice and modern as it circled the airfield. Bill felt a wave of confidence run through his body. He had hoped he would not be expected to fly in some old type of machine like a Bombay, or other equally ancient contraption. So he was pleasantly surprised that he was to embark in a Hudson of the latest type.

The big plane made a perfect landing and taxied across the field to a place near the hangars. A door in the side of the machine opened, and about sixteen people got out. They were chiefly officers coming to visit the front, and men of the R.A.F., changing station. After the passengers had alighted, luggage and mail were unloaded. Bill was surprised to see how much these machines were capable of carrying.

In a remarkably short time, the unloading was completed and the plane loaded up again with luggage and mails for the return journey. Finally, the Transport officer gave permission for the passengers to emplane.

Bill clambered inside and sat down on one side of the long shaped, small room for passengers. You had to sit sideways, and there wasn't much chance of seeing through the few small circular windows unless you twisted yourself round on your seat and bent down to peer out. There was a door at the top end leading to the pilot's compartment, where the two pilots sat; also the Wireless Operator and the Navigator.

There wasn't a seat left when finally the door was shut and snibbed. There were several officers, three of four N.C.O.'s and about five Rank and File of the R.A.F. The rear portion of the plane was packed up to the roof with mails and parcels of every description.

The pilots came in, clambered over everybody's legs, their door was shut, and the engines started up. It wasn't nearly as noisy as Bill had expected, even when the engines were reeved up as they taxied across the airfield.

Just for a moment, Bill felt an insane desire to leap up and jump out of the machine. He felt trapped, and wanted to get away to the safety of terra firma. But he took a firm grip of himself, and laughed under his breath.

The machine stopped at the end of the run and turned into the wind. The pilot opened up each engine in turn, and then let it slow down again, to see that all was well. The door of the forward compartment opened and one of the pilots put his head through the opening.

"Will you all please come forward as far as possible for the take-off?" he said, and the passengers moved up as close together as they could.

Bill looked at his watch. In another minute they would be in the air. The engines opened up with a roar, and the machine started to gather speed across the airfield. It was rather like being in a train, and the ground outside sped past at an ever-increasing pace. There were many bumps, then an appreciable interval, then a last one and they were in the air. Men standing on the airfield began to look smaller, and the hangars sped past the windows into the distance. There was really no sensation of flying at all. One might just as well have been sitting in a bus, travelling at high speed along the Great North Road. The machine banked steeply, and, coming slowly back to an even keel, headed away Eastwards up over the foothills. Far below, Bill could see tiny flocks of goats feeding on the scanty grass of the hillside.

It was a glorious day, with hardly any wind, so the aircraft flew pretty steadily. By watching the tips of the wings against the horizon, Bill could tell how steadily they were flying. He had been too interested to worry about his own feelings so far. Now he was up in the air, and it wasn't so bad after all. He knew that he was not going to be ill, and set himself to enjoy the novelty of the journey.

As soon as they had crossed the hills, the plane came down to a very low altitude, and started to skim over the surface of the ground like a gigantic swallow. Bill turned to an R.A.F. officer sitting beside him and asked why they were flying so low.

"For safety," was the reply. "Any lurking Junkers 88 would find it very difficult to see us from up above if we keep low. You don't want to be shot down, do you?"

"Not exactly," replied Bill. He felt a qualm of uneasiness pass through him. He hadn't thought of any danger from the Luftwaffe so far away from the battle front. But after all, the Germans sent reconnaissance planes as far away as Cairo, so it was quite on the cards that they might get attacked at any time during the journey. The flight suddenly seemed to be a very long one. It would take them six hours before they put down at Almaza. Since he had brought nothing to read with him, there was nothing to do but to think of something else, and make an effort not to look at his watch too often.

Bill did the next best thing, he tried to lull himself to sleep. He must have succeeded, for the next thing he saw was an airfield far beneath him, and the plane was banking steeply as they circled above it.

"Where are we?" he asked the R.A.F. officer beside him.

"El Adem. We're just going to land. The slits are down." He motioned Bill to look out of the window at the back portion of the wings. There were six tubular pieces of metal set at intervals along the wings; the air brakes. Flat pieces of metal started to come out slowly from underneath each slot. As they fell into position, the aircraft visibly slowed down, and the earth started to come up at them, but not so quickly as to make it unpleasant. Bill had heard so many stories about the nastiness of coming down that he was quite prepared to be worried by the sensation. But there was no sensation at all. The earth just came nearer and nearer until, at last, they appeared to be skimming at great speed across the surface of the airfield. Then there came a bump, followed quite slowly by another, then a succession of small bumps and they were rolling heavily across the sands of the aerodrome. The speed slackened, and the sensation was the same as it had been at the take-off. Bill heaved an inward sigh of relief. They were down.

All the passengers clambered out for a breather in the fresh air outside. The cessation of noise was a great relief.

Bill lit a cigarette and walked round the machine. He laughed to himself. If that was all there was to it, there was nothing in flying after all. He registered a vow to bring a book with him the next time he had to travel by air. Without something to read the whole process was merely boring.

They only waited long enough to take on fuel and drop any mails for El Adem, then they took off for the short trip to Gambut. The skipper of the plane was a young man of Imperial Airways who had many hundreds of flying hours to his credit. When he heard that Bill Wilson was making his maiden trip in an aircraft, he asked him to come up into the nose of the plane and sit beside him as they flew. Bill went forward as they took off from Gambut, and found it far more pleasant sitting up there than in the stuffy compartment with the passengers. He had a magnificent view through the windows in the nose, far better than peering through the stupid little ones in the side of the fusilage. The pilots had a plentiful stock of chicken, ham, and egg sandwiches and all were offered to him. Then a cup of really good coffee, and to crown it all, an orange. Bill had been living on bully-beef and hard biscuits ever since the beginning of the battle, and to be regaled with this sumptuous fare was a treat indeed. It started him thinking of the bath he would have immediately they landed at Cairo, to be rapidly followed by the best dinner that 'Jimmy's' Restaurant could provide.

The pilot was an excellent chap, and when Bill asked if they would fly across the battlefields, he decided to make a short detour to take them over the field of El Alamein. They were then flying over the lovely bay at Capuzzo, heading away Westwards along the line of the railway towards Alexandria. The sun was getting low in the sky, and Bill could not bring himself to believe that they could possibly reach the airport before dark. On the ground, it had taken him seven hours all out in a fast car to cover the same distance, and here they were proposing to do it in under one hour. It didn't seem possible, somehow. But it wasn't any of his business, the pilots doubtless knew what they were about!

Below him, he could see thousands of small holes in the ground where men had dug themselves in during the heat of the battle. It was amazing how clearly each little hole appeared when viewed from the air. All his preconceived ideas of concealment from aeroplanes went by the board. It seemed possible to see just everything from the air. So what was the use of trying to hide anything at all? Colours seemed to be the only way of dealing satisfactorily with the problem.

They flew over Daba and on towards El Alamein. The sea stretched away into the distance as far as the eye could see. Beneath them, there was little evidence that one of the decisive battles of the War had been fought out on those sandy stretches. Apart from the many small holes in the ground, there was absolutely nothing to be seen at all. The plane veered round a little bit to the Southward, and they left the sea and struck directly across the desert in the direction of Cairo. Away to the South was the rugged markings of the Quattara Depression, that impassable barrier of rocks and sand which had brought Rommel's hordes to a definite standstill last August. Not even German ingenuity could enable vehicles to get across those rugged rocks and silt.

They picked up the Wadi Natrun just as the sun was starting to set, and Bill could see the Alexandria road stretching like a black ribbon far beneath him. Small toy cars were clearly visible speeding in both directions. He laughed to himself when he thought that he would be lying in a hot bath in a comfortable hotel long before any of these cars could hope to reach Cairo.

On they flew towards the greenery of the Nile Delta. The change from the Desert to the cultivation of the Nile basin was a very sudden one. One moment they were flying across sandy desert, and the next the ground below was a mass of trees and green fields, with little villages dotted here and there among the foliage. Ahead of them were the lights and buildings of the Egyptian Capital. Bill felt that he was leaving the war behind him and travelling on this Magic Carpet to a land of delight, peopled by head waiters and pretty girls on dance floors. He might be here to see the Doctors, but he was determined to have as good a time as possible.

"Airfield in sight." The second pilot spoke to the Wireless Operator, who smiled and packed up his instrument. They flew on over Heliopolis and circled the airfield preparatory to landing. The young pilot told Bill to stand behind him as they came down, so that he could see what happened when a plane landed.

Bill stood up, the second pilot took his place beside the man in charge. The air brakes went out, and the machine felt as if it were stopping in the air. They veered round and headed straight for the landing ground ahead. The houses came up to meet them, and Bill thought that the aerodrome at Almaza looked so small that they might well fail to hit it, and crash against some of the houses. Nearer and nearer rose the rooftops. Bill wondered if they would be able to clear them. The nearest roof felt almost touchable as they passed over it, then they were skimming along the runway a few feet above the ground. The nose came up, and the engines throttled right down. There was a series of small bumps followed by the heavy rolling of the rubber tyres on the hard surface of the aerodrome. Gradually their speed slackened, and the big plane rumbled across the ground in the direction of the hangars. They were down; safety at last! Now for the Continental Hotel and a good wallow in a bath!

They alighted from the plane and found a lorry waiting to convey all the passengers and their luggage into the middle of Cairo. Bill was very lucky, and managed to get a room before they were all booked up. Another ten minutes, and he was lying in all the luxury of a very hot bath, filled to the brim. The very feeling of having four walls round about him was a pleasant novelty. There was no question but that he would enjoy his evening.

* * *

Bill Wilson never forgot that wonderful evening, the first one spent in civilisation after several months of life in the Desert. He went downstairs after his bath, and had a few welcome drinks at the hotel bar. The clear soda water in the whisky went down exceedingly well after the salty water of the Battalion Mess back in the Desert. He was in battle-dress, having nothing else to wear, and on his shoulders was the famous 'HD' sign of the Highland Division. Evidently the Division was now famous after the battle reports in the Press, and Bill was soon surrounded by brother officers who had been either wounded or evacuated sick, all clamouring for news of their friends up the line. One Captain Murdoch Fraser, a gunner, had been at school with Bill. He had been hit in the arm by a shell splinter early on in the battle, and sent back to the Delta. Now he was on sick leave prior to rejoining his unit.

Bill found that Fraser was not engaged for the evening, so he suggested that they both went round the corner to the St. James Restaurant, commonly known as 'Jimmy's'. Fraser readily agreed, and a few minutes later they were seated at a small table in a corner of the restaurant.

"What are we going to eat, Bill?" asked Fraser. "I don't suppose you've tasted decent food for the devil of a long time."

"You're right there, Murdoch," laughed Bill. "I've been living on bully beef, biscuits and jam for ages and ages. Come on then, let's have a real blow-out. Waiter!"

A waiter hovered round them with the menu card, and Bill ordered what Murdoch called a grand dinner.

Bill Wilson looked round the well-known place. Nothing had changed since the last time he had dined there, some weeks before the battle of Alamein. There were perhaps more Americans about, but substantially the place was unaltered. There were the same parties of officers and their lady friends, and the same Egyptians and Greeks. The general atmosphere of the room was that of comfortable eating. There certainly did not seem to be any shortage of food, and it was difficult to imagine that there was a war on at all, save for the fact that most of the men were in uniform of some kind or other.

The dinner arrived. It was a most pleasant meal, and Bill Wilson found it a great treat just to sit there in decent surroundings and enjoy the amenities of civilisation. It might only be an interlude, but it was a very pleasant one.

After lingering over their brandy and coffee, they decided to move on to the Continental Cabaret. They left the restaurant, went back to the hotel and sat watching the dancers till close on mid-night. Then Bill felt that he had had a long enough day, and, bidding Murdoch Fraser good-night, went up to his room and to bed. He had hardly laid his head on the pillow before he was in a deep, dreamless slumber.

The interview with the eye specialist wasn't nearly as bad as Bill had expected. He had been haunted with the fear that he had done some permanent damage to his sight, and that it might possibly interfere with his future career as a Regular Soldier. The Army was his bread and butter, and without his health, he was of no use to anyone. The doctor spared no pains to get to the root of the trouble. The upshot of it all was that there was no organic damage and that all could be put right with a new set of glasses. Bill felt enormously relieved. He was assured that when he had grown accustomed to the new glasses, all should be well. But it would take a week or two before the eyes settled down again.

He took the prescription to a shop and was told that they could be ready in three days time. He went off to G.H.Q. to book a passage in an aircraft the day after he had collected the new glasses. That done, there was nothing left but to enjoy himself as best he could for the intervening period. Many of his friends up in the Desert had asked him to do little pieces of shopping for them. The days were spent in roving round the shops, and the evenings in dining with his many friends who happened to be in Cairo at the moment. He would have very much liked to go to the Pictures, but he dared not risk doing any more damage to his eyes.

The time passed all too quickly, and almost before he realised it, Bill found himself getting up at the unearthly hour of half past three in the morning to catch the bus at four for Almaza Airport. It was still dark when he clambered into the waiting Hudson, and the runways of the aerodrome were all floodlit to enable them to take off in the darkness.

He did not feel any apprehension this time, he had by now complete confidence in the pilots, and was certain that he was not going to be ill in the air.

There were not so many passengers as on the downward journey. There were several Air Force and about six Army Officers, together with three sergeants of an infantry regiment, flying back to re-join their unit. It was bitterly cold outside, and Bill was thankful to be in the warm interior of the aeroplane.

The engines roared, and the big plane taxied across the airfield to the end of the runway. Here it stopped for the scheduled testing of each of the motors. The engines reeved up and the machine gathered speed in the darkness. There were the usual bumps at gradually increasing intervals, until they were in the air.

Looking out of the windows, Bill could see the dim lights of Cairo a long way below. Very soon these faded out altogether, and they were left in utter darkness.

It was not for another half hour that the dawn came up. Gradually the whole sky got lighter and lighter, and then, at last, the sun broke out from beneath the horizon, like a ball of fire. This sunrise over the Desert, seen from the air, was one of the most beautiful sights Bill Wilson had ever witnessed. But the beauty did not last long, for they ran into clouds shortly after sunrise, and before they landed at El Adem, it was raining hard. It cleared up again before they got to Benina, from where he had set forth only four short days before. His driver was there to meet him, and in a few minutes they were on the road, speeding in the direction of Benghazi. They had a fairly clear road for most of the way, and ended up by driving into the battalion lines well beyond Agedabia at five o'clock in the afternoon.

It was almost incredible to think that he had slept some of the previous night in far off Cairo. Here he was back again, once more, in the middle of the Lybian Desert. Back to the sand and the discomforts, back to the bully beef and biscuits, back to the salty water in the whisky. Bill smiled to himself. He had had a good time, and his mind had been set at ease about his eyes. But, best of all, he was back again among the friends he liked the most. Feeling thoroughly contented with his lot, he dismissed the car and went off in search of tea.

CHAPTER XI

CHRISTMAS

THE EXPECTED BATTLE AT MERSA BREGA NEVER developed at all. For a couple of weeks, all concerned had been busying themselves in getting ready for the big attack. Infantry patrols were sent out every night to find out as much as they could about the dispositions of the enemy. The Inverness Regiment was one of the battalions in the line during the last few days, and they came in for a good deal of this patrol work. Colonel Forsyth would lie for hours at a time in the sand dunes, studying his front through field-glasses. About two miles away, he could see figures of Italian soldiers come out from the small fort above the harbour of Mersa Brega and go down to the beach to bathe, and wash their clothes. He studied the lie of the land ahead, and worked out how he would advance when the attack started. He even accompanied some of the patrols which went out every night.

The country in front of the Inverness Regiment's position was fairly flat, but there were many small deceptive hollows in the dunes which might well hold small packets of enemy defenders. Patrols were always fired upon, and they were thus able to pin-point quite a number of the enemy strong points.

There was a good deal of shelling. The Germans appeared to have concentrated a considerable quantity of their artillery on a relatively narrow front. The small field guns weren't so bad, but the two hundred and five millimetre guns were a little disconcerting. You could hear their shells coming at you like an express train, and they made a huge crater wherever they landed. But the Germans must have been pretty short of ammunition, since they did not fire these big fellows more than a few times each day.

On the night before the advance was due to begin, patrols were sent out as usual. They crawled out as far as they had ever been on any previous night, but could not manage to draw any fire from the enemy posts in No man's Land. In the early hours of the morning, when the reports were consolidated after all the patrols had returned, it became obvious what had happened. The enemy had withdrawn, and the village of Mersa Brega was untenanted.

Reconnaissance parties were at once sent out to ascertain the true position, and as a result, a pursuit force of infantry and tanks was got together and plans were hastily made to follow up after the retreating enemy.

But, as the old Scots saying has it, 'The best laid schemes of mice and men gang eft agley'. The Germans had made such a good job of mining the road and the surrounding country, that any idea of immediate pursuit was out of the question. For days on end, the Engineers laboured at lifting these mines, at considerable cost in men. By the time the road was safe as far as Agheila, the New Zealanders, who were carrying on the pursuit by way of the Desert route, were some hundred miles farther on, still in touch with the retreating enemy. The appreciation was that Rommel would not again try to make a stand until he had got back to the vicinity of the Wadi Chebir. This meant that there would be a period of planning and preparation. It would not be possible to send forward big bodies of troops and vehicles until the 'Q' Services had got forward an adequate scale of supplies, ammunition and petrol. The Highlanders had to be content with sitting down at Agheila for a couple of weeks, and this was eventually much appreciated by all concerned, for it gave them a chance to lick their sores, and to spend both Christmas and the New Year under reasonably comfortable conditions.

On Christmas Eve, young Walter Mitchell, the Signal officer was sitting in his dug-out talking to John Gray and Hamish Macdonald. They had had a long day of inspections and training. The little dug-out was nothing more than a hole in the ground, just sufficient to take a single camp bed with a small space at one side to allow the occupant to move about. The roof was made of a canvas shelter, supported by small poles of wood stuck into the sides of the walls. All three young officers were sitting on Walter's bed, smoking his last cigarettes. It was getting dark outside, and they were not allowed to smoke in the open for fear of giving the position away to enemy aircraft. The dug-out was the only place to smoke.

"Have either of you blokes heard if the turkey has arrived yet?" enquired Walter.

"I asked the Major a few minutes ago," said John Gray. "He said it hadn't come yet."

"The Jocks won't half be mad if it doesn't turn up after all," grinned Hamish. "They've been promised a decent Christmas dinner, and there'll be awful disappointment if it doesn't materialise."

"Don't you think it's asking too much, Hamish," said Walter, "to get turkey and plum-pudding here in the middle of the ruddy Western Desert?"

"I agree it's a bit of a marvel, but after all, they've promised the beastly stuff. It's a bad show to raise all our hopes and then not be able to do anything about it. Have any of you trusting officers got a cigarette? I'm absolutely out of them."

"Have one of these," said John Gray, holding out a battered packet of Victory 'V's. "I've got a few left here."

"Thanks awfully, old son. I'll repay you some day, when I get a fresh supply."

"That'll probably be in Tripoli," laughed Walter, "if and when we ever get there. We seem to be stuck here for the duration. Has either of you two heard any talk of our making a move forward?"

"Not a word," said Hamish, puffing luxuriously at his cigarette. "But I expect that we shall soon be off again. It's not like the Army Commander to sit down for very long at a time."

"I wish to heaven we could get on with it," said John. "I'm sick of this Desert. What on earth the Germans wanted the place for at all beats me."

"They didn't want the Desert, idiot," said Walter. "They wanted to get Egypt and the Suez Canal.

They couldn't get those without coming through the Desert."

"Yes, I know all that. But Mussolini wanted to have all this long before the War was even thought of. Who in the world would want to live in these parts ? I can't believe that even the Arabs like the place. I suppose they stay here just because they don't know of anything else."

"Benghazi wouldn't be too bad under peace conditions," said John.

"Perhaps so, but I don't think I want to be stationed there after the war is over. I'd far rather be taken for the occupied territories. It would be much more fun living in Germany with the Army of Occupation than being cooped up here in Benghazi or Tripoli, or some such outlandish place. Don't you think so, Hamish ?"

"We'll none of us get the chance of doing either," laughed Hamish. "As soon as this party is over, we'll all be winkled off to the Far East to fight those rotten Little Men. You see if we don't. It'll be perfectly beastly, fighting in tropical jungles and swamps and things. I think I'd rather stop here in the Desert."

"Nobody wants to go off and fight against the Japs," said Walter. "We all want to get home as soon as Germany has been beaten. But it won't work out like that. Somebody has to go out there and beat the little beggars. We've all the experience, and so I don't see how they would get along without us."

"Surely we'll bomb Japan in a big way," put in Hamish. "They'll never be able to stand up to the combined Air Forces of the United Nations. Tokio would burst into flames if you dropped a few incendiary bombs on it. The place is only made of paper, after all. My! Wouldn't it burn!"

"Have you ever thought how far away Japan is?" asked Walter. "I mean to say, the nearest aerodromes in Siberia are more than a hundred miles further from Tokio than London is from Berlin. It's not as easy as you think to bomb Japan."

"Don't be depressing, you two," said John Gray, with a laugh. "After all, it is Christmas Eve. We jolly well ought to get drunk to-night, if there was anything to get drunk with. Has the Mess got any hooch left, do you know?"

"I know that they have been keeping a little on ice for to-morrow night," said Walter. The Black Watch had about twenty cases of Glen Grant sent out here the other day. But I expect those will be very much for home consumption. Still, as we have a few distinguished visitors coming to-morrow night, I think they might be persuaded to unbuckle a few bottles for the occasion. I hope the Major has asked them. It would be a bit dull to eat one's Christmas dinner without any drink at all."

"I hope the promised bottles of beer for the men arrive in time," said Hamish. "It would make all the difference to them."

"Yes, I'll say it would," remarked Walter. "And if by any lucky chance there was a delivery of mails as well, that would just round the thing nicely off for them. Let's hope something does turn up."

There was a shout outside the dug-out. "Is young John Gray in there?"

"Yes. Who's that?" replied John, peering through the doorway of the bivouac.

A face appeared in the entrance. It was Michael Watson, the Captain of 'A' Company. "Come along out here, young John," he said with a grin. "The Christmas dinners have arrived at Brigade and I want you to take a truck and go down to get them."

Shouts of satisfaction came from the three youngsters in the dug-out. "What's coming along?" asked Walter.

"I don't know all about it, but I hear there is turkey, pork, Christmas pudding and a bottle of beer for each man. And into the bargain, I believe there is a batch of mail in at the same time. Looks like being a pretty decent Christmas after all."

"Oh boy! Am I off in a hurry," laughed John Gray, and disappeared in the direction of his platoon lines, in search of a truck to collect the precious Christmas fare.

* * *

It was the hour before dinner, and most of the Signals officers had gathered in their little Mess to discuss the events of the day, and the possibilities of the Christmas fare arriving in time for the morrow. The Mess President, Major Greig, had seen to it that there was a reasonable quantity of drinks put by to tide them over the festive period. They had all done without for the last two weeks, in order that there should be something at Christmas. A dry Christmas wouldn't have suited them.

"Are we allowed to break our long fast now, James?" asked the Colonel, as he came into the tent.

"I had not blown the whistle until you came, Sir," laughed Major Greig. "Baker! You can open up now, and bring me a large whisky to begin with. What about you, Sir?"

"I'll have one too, Baker, thank you," said the Colonel, sitting down beside the wireless set. "Anything on the News this evening?"

"Things don't appear to be going any too well in North Africa," remarked Alec Foster. "They're being held up a bit there."

"It'll be a great day when we join up with those blokes, Sir," chimed in Douglas Macdonald from the other end of the Mess. "Do you think we'll be able to get letters any faster after we've joined forces?"

"It certainly ought to make a world of difference. I've had no letter from home for about three weeks now. Have you chaps had any lately?"

"I had one last week, Sir," said Foster. "But it was only a bill."

"You wouldn't pay it anyway, Alec," grinned James Carter.

"Speak for yourself, James," Alec retorted. "I only wish it had been a bill from your firm; except that I don't patronise you very much. I value the places where I invest my money too much to do anything so silly as that."

"The ingratitude of man!" snorted Major Carter. "After all the expert advice I've tendered you in the past as to the legal hours of drinking and getting a meal in every ostlery in Scotland." Major Carter was a very well-known lawyer in civil life, and prided himself in his knowledge of little-known laws relating to Inns and Hotels.

"I'll remember you in my will, James," laughed Foster. "This whisky tastes good, doesn't it, you chaps?"

"A decent rest from alcoholic stimulants has done you people a world of good," grinned the Colonel. "You'd only drink yourselves to death if you got the chance."

"And a very pleasant death too," put in James Greig, helping himself to another nip out of the bottle.

"I hear the Christmas fare has arrived after all, James," said the Colonel to Major Greig. "When are you going to collect it?"

"I've a lorry down at Rear Division just now, Sir, waiting for the stuff. It should be back almost any moment now."

"What are we getting, James?" asked Carter.

"There's turkey, goose, ham, plum-pudding and cake. And also a bottle of beer for every man."

"That sounds all right," remarked the Colonel. "Are the officers getting anything like the same sumptuous fare?"

"Just the same, Sir. And I've managed to set aside six bottles of whisky and four of gin. But these will have to do for both, Christmas and Hogmanay. We won't be able to get any more now."

"I think you've done very well indeed, James. What time are you giving the men their meal? Midday or in the evening?"

"About four in the afternoon, Sir. There's to be a football match at two o'clock, and the dinners will be ready for them afterwards, at about four. The men will all feed by Sections, as usual. By having it at four, there will be plenty of time for them to finish up before it gets dark. Oh, and there's twenty cigarettes for every man. They're doing very well out of it."

"Yes," remarked Alec Foster. "I think it's a jolly good show on the part of all the Supply people that they've managed to bring the stuff to the troops out here in the blue, at exactly the right time. It must have all been laid on months ago. Think of the organisation it must have involved."

"I agree," said the Colonel. "It's a great show on the part of all concerned. We must see that it's decently cocked, and that every man gets his fair share."

"There'll be no fear about that, Sir," said James Greig. "We've got it all organised to the last detail."

"The lads deserve a decent meal for a change," said the Colonel, rising to his feet. "They've certainly earned all we can give them. Ah well! I must away to my dinner. I'll probably look in later on as usual. Don't drink all the whisky, you thirsty blighters!"

With that he left the Mess tent and went back to his own dug-out for a wash before he walked across to the Divisional Mess where he always fed.

* * *

It was Christmas night, and dinner was nearly over in the Divisional Headquarters Mess. The Signals Colonel leant back in his chair and surveyed the scene. He was sitting at one end of the long table around which some fifteen officers were seated, packed as close together as sardines. There was one brilliant electric light bulb in the middle of the roof, worked off the Division's portable lighting set.

The day had been a good one, and all those who could manage to do so had observed it as a holiday. There had been the usual visits round the Sergeants and Warrant Officers, and in the afternoon several football matches. Then had come the men's dinners, and Colonel Denman and Major Carter had done the rounds of their Sections to see that all was well with the magnificent meal served out to the men. Teetotalers were the most popular people in the camp that afternoon! Bottles of beer were exchanged for packets of cigarettes. There was enough and to spare for every man, and by the time that darkness fell over the desert, every one of them was feeling pleasantly satisfied with life, at any rate, for a bit.

The Colonel was sitting next to Colonel Evans, the ADOS* of the Division, and opposite him was the visit-

---

* Assistant Director of Ordnance Services.

ing General's ADC. The Corps Commander was the guest of the evening, although there were several others interspersed between the regular members of the Mess. They had just drunk the Royal Toast, and the coffee was being served. Outside, the piper was tuning up his pipes, preparatory to the traditional ceremony in Scottish Messes.

Colonel Evans turned to his companion. "Did you ever hear my story of how I became an ADOS?" He said with a smile.

"My dear Admirable ADOS," said Colonel Denman. "If you've told me that story once, you've told it a hundred times, but only when under the influence of alcohol."

"Under these circumstances I might perhaps spare you listening to it again."

"I fear you'll have to, here comes the piper. I trust, as an Englishman, that you'll enjoy the performance."

"All the cats in the world howling together," remarked Evans, as the piper entered the little room. He was dressed in the kilt of a famous Highland Regiment, and a simple battle-dress blouse. He was only a youngster, but he played the pipes magnificently. Round and round that small table he marched, playing the old tunes of the Homeland. The conversation died down completely, and from the faces of the officers, one could see their thoughts were far away, away back in their native Scotland, absorbed in this music of the Clans of old.

The piper came in and out, playing several different tunes each time, but going out for a short rest between entrances. Then he came back and stopped beside the General's chair. The GOC poured out a small wine-glass of whisky and handed it to the Corps Commander. He in turn handed it to the piper who, standing stiffly to attention, gave the old Gaelic toast which means "Good health, and gentlemen present". Then he turned smartly to his right and marched out of the room.

After a brief pause, he came back again and played whatever tunes the guests asked him to play. Reels and Strathspeys, Laments and Marches — they were all the same to him.

Then the table and chairs were taken outside, and the place prepared for an Eightsome Reel. No Scottish Mess worthy of the name would let Christmas go by without dancing a reel, and they were certainly not going to let a little thing like the Western Desert stop them on this occasion. The four officers chosen to dance were the Corps Commander, the GOC, the ADMS, and Colonel Denman. The other four were the CRA, the G1, the ADC and Colonel Evans. There was precious little room, especially for the two Generals, who were both well over six feet tall. But they managed it somehow, to the strains of the piper playing in the little doorway. It was a cold night, but all eight officers were in a healthy state of perspiration when the dance ended.

The next move was to attend a performance of the Divisional Concert Party, who were giving a show nearby. Their stage had been rigged up in the middle of four large lorries. It had been done so cleverly that, once inside, you could hardly tell that you were not in a small theatre. There were little sketches and Scottish comedians, conjurers and funny men. The audience forgot that they were in the Desert and thoroughly enjoyed themselves. It was a really first-class show, and no charge had been made for admission to any of the soldiers. At the end of the performance, the Corps Commander made a little speech, and the whole company joined hands to sing Auld Lang Syne, although it wasn't yet New Year's Night.

The visitors said good-night, and Colonel Denman strolled across to his own Signals Mess to see what was going on there. He heard the strains of the pipes coming from the tent as he approached, there was a party in progress. As he entered he was hailed with shouts.

All the Signals officers were there, seated round the table, and on the edges of the shallow trench in which the tent stood. On a chair at one side sat Captain Bill Wilson, who commanded No. 2 Company, playing away lustily on his pipes. He was a bonny piper, and had been Pipe-major of his OTC band when he was at school in Edinburgh. He stopped playing, got up and came forward with his hand outstretched.

"A merry Christmas to you, Sir," he said. "And many of them."

"The same to you, Bill. I suppose you have the drink taken? You ought to have by now, anyway.

Is there anything left for me, or have you finished the lot?"

"Here you are, Sir," said young Craig, who commanded the Cable Section. And he handed the Colonel a bottle of whisky.

"I really don't know where you fellows get the stuff," remarked the Colonel, as he helped himself, and filled his glass up with some brackish-looking water out of a jug standing on the table.

"What sort of a dinner did you have?" Asked Major Carter.

"Not too bad at all. But we only had pork, and I believe you lucky devils had turkey. Is that so?"

"Oh, yes. We never do things by halves here," said James Greig.

"What about a tune, Bill?" The Colonel turned to Wilson, who was twisting the drones of his pipes. "Give us the 'Green Hills of Tyrol'."

"Right you are, Sir. Here we go." He tuned up and started to play what was always the Colonel's favourite pipe tune. Wilson played it excellently.

The sound of the pipes had the result it never-failingly has on any Scotsman, wherever he may be. The tune lifted them up and carried them back to far-off Scotland, back to the land of the heather and the hills. Back to the little country of mists and rain, to the sound of the sheep on the hillside and the 'Whoop' of the curlew in the morning sky. These men had come through the heat of modern battle, they had sailed across the seas in hourly peril of death from drowning. They had endured much on the battlefield of El Alamein, and had every right to feel embittered and hardened to modern warfare. But the wailing song of the bagpipes took them back across the intervening seas to their native land, back to the scenes of their childhood. Till Wilson finished, they all sat spellbound, captivated by this wonderful music which had so great an appeal to their Scottish hearts.

"Well done, old son," said the Colonel.

"Have a wee drappie after all yon."

"I will that, Sir, thank you." And Wilson helped himself to a generous measure from the now sadly depleted bottle.

And so they talked, and listened to the playing of the pipes until the small hours. Then, one by one, they departed to their beds in the sand. The Colonel and Major Carter were the last to leave the Mess.

"I wonder where we shall all be this time next year," he mused as they stood for a moment in the entrance, before saying good-night.

"In Scotland, pray God," said Carter with a smile.

"There's no harm in hoping. — Anyway, I'm off to my bed."

"So am I, Sir. Good-night to you."

"Good-night, James. Pleasant dreams."

They parted and went their various ways.

CHAPTER XII

THE WADI CHEBIR

THE HIGHLANDERS REMAINED IN THE VICINITY OF El Agheila until after the New Year. There were the traditional celebrations of Hogmanay, but it was only for a very few hours that they allowed themselves the relaxation of celebrations. Hard exercises were the order of the day. They all knew that this was only an interlude, and that there was much stern fighting ahead of them. News came filtering back that Rommel was preparing a position in the area beyond the Wadi Chebir, the rugged strip of country West of the village of Buerat, inland from the coast.

Day after day, night after night, they practiced assiduously, even as they had done before the battle of El Alamein. Engineers did all they could to teach the rest of the army how to recognise and remove enemy mines of all sorts. The infantry marched and dug, marched and dug, and gave the men little chance to get soft. There was fighting to be done, and they were going to be ready for it when it came along.

About the tenth of the month, John Gray of the Inverness Regiment found himself once more on the move with his platoon. They were in lorries of an RASC* company, and the whole Regiment was to be transported up the line towards Sirte, where the forward troops were in contact with Rommel's retreating

---
* Royal Army Service Corps.

forces. It was a boring journey, and took them up the long, straight coast road for mile after dusty mile. They reached Marble Arch on the afternoon of the first day out from El Agheila, and John was surprised to see the extent of this great airfield. It seemed to stretch for miles, and was littered with aircraft of all shapes and sizes, especially those great Douglas American machines, which had been travelling over their heads in both directions for several days past, carrying petrol and supplies to the New Zealanders up forward.

They passed underneath the great Marble Arch, erected by the Italians to show that they were the true descendants of the great Roman Empire of days gone by. In actual fact, the original Marble Arch was erected by the Phoenicians, to mark the spot where a great walking race ended. Two brothers accepted the challenge of the people living on the other side of the boundary, to walk from the far side of their kingdom in the direction of Marble Arch. The boundary was to be erected at the place where the competitors met. Nobody would believe that the brothers had not run, so far did they manage to get before they met the men from the other side. However, the onlookers decided that they would believe them if they agreed to let themselves be buried alive on the spot, as a proof of their honesty. They agreed, and were duly buried on the scene of their triumph, that their country might be the richer by their sacrifice. A grateful people erected a monument over the place where they were buried, and this is the site of the Marble Arch of the present day. John Gray thought it rather a pity that Mussolini had not won a similar race at that spot.

It would have saved the world such a lot of trouble, and would probably have given him as much publicity as he wanted, without having to plunge his wretched country into a war.

They bivouaced for the night outside Nofilia, a bleak, outlandish spot on the edge of the desert. Just before dark, the usual little fires leapt up on all sides, denoting that the Regiment was 'brewing up' it's evening meal. All over the camping ground small groups of men were gathered round little scrapes in the ground where petrol tins filled with sand and sprinkled with petrol provided a very quick and handy method of raising a fire to prepare the tea so dear to the heart of the British soldier. The food was chiefly bully beef, or the more acceptable 'M and V', (meat and veg.). Of bread, there was none, and the eternal biscuits were the only form of flour which they ever taw. Earlier in the battle, when they had been nearer so the fleshpots of Egypt, there had been an occasional issue of white bread. But now, many hundreds of miles from their Base, the soldier had to put up with biscuits at every meal in the day. They weren't too bad, and many a man found that he had come to like these hard articles of kitchen ware almost as he had liked his bread in the old days.

Soon after dark, the Germans came over and bombed the airfield at Nofilia. This was a good two miles from the place where the Inverness Regiment camped. But the planes dropped several flares too near them to be healthy, and these had to be shot out with rifle and light machine-gun fire. No bombs were dropped anywhere near their camp, and the raid only lasted for a few minutes. After it was over, the men went back to their blankets and were soon sound asleep.

They were well out on the road again by eight o'clock in the morning, and took to the desert on leaving Nofilia. Their route lead them inland, and they drove for mile after mile across rolling downs. It had been the same between Derna and Benghazi, except that there had been a pretty decent road, and here only a mere sand track, marked out by the vehicles which had gone on before them. It was a weary stretch, and many of the men fell asleep as they rode.

The battalion had to spend one more night on the journey. This time, they stopped right out in the desert, in the vicinity of Sultan. It was not at all like the desert they had known, as there were no undulations, and little or no cover. For mile after mile, there was absolutely nothing but flat, stony ground. To dig slit trenches would have meant blasting operations in the solid rock. They spent the night unmolested, and set off once again as soon as it was light.

About noon, the leading company passed through the little village of Sirte, a pretty place, studded with green palm trees and small white houses. There were several notices bearing the ominous words *'Danger — mines — Keep out'*, so there was no wandering into the attractive looking side streets, even if they had been able to stop to do so.

After passing through Sirte, their road took them along a dead straight stretch beside the sea. On the right were undulating sand dunes, and on the left was the stone desert, stretching away as far as the eye could see, in a dead flat plain. Along the road were notices with the words 'This road is bombed — Keep your interval of 200 yards between vehicles'. There had been several instances lately of enemy fighters sweeping along the roadway shooting up transport, and a Colonel from Corps Headquarters had met his death just outside Buerat village. He had been driving his car himself, when two fighters came swooping down from the East, firing their guns as the same time. The Colonel had jammed on the brakes and made as if to jump out of the car, but just as he was about to make his leap, another fighter plane, coming up from the opposite direction, poured a stream of bullets into his back. He was killed instantly, but his two companions managed to get away.

The Inverness Regiment made the journey to camping ground beyond Tamet airfield without any such unpleasant incident, and here they found that they had been allocated a very nice stretch of sand dunes on the seaward side of the main road. John Gray was allotted a small area near the last line of sand hills for his platoon, and he immediately set his men to dig themselves in, as was their invariable habit whenever they stopped at the end of a march. Each pair of men dug themselves an oblong slit in the ground over which they erected two canvas bivouacs which had been fixed together. The result was a very comfortable shelter for two, where both could lie with their bodies under the surface of the earth for protection and warmth, and underneath the cover of the bivouac to keep the morning's heavy dew from soaking them as they slept. Such were the holes in which the men of the Eighth Army lived.

John Gray had just finished his own little home with the help of his batman, when up strolled young Walter Mitchell who had come on ahead with the Advance Party the day before.

"Hullo, John," said Walter, sitting down on the edge of the hole, and lighting a cigarette. "What sort of a run did you have?"

"Not too bad, old son," replied John, stripping off his shirt for his evening wash in the mere trickle of water which the daily ration of one gallon per man allowed him to use. "They bombed the aerodrome at Nofilia when we were there, but nobody was hurt."

"We had a bit of excitement here yesterday," said Walter with a little laugh. "It was just after we had arrived, and we hadn't had time to dig any slit trenches. About twenty Jerry bombers flew in from the sea, just over this place, and dropped their eggs on Tamet airfield. As they were making off the way they had come, their escort of about ten fighters dived down and came back along the main road at about fifty feet. They blazed away at some lorries, and managed to knock out three, about a mile away from here. I didn't like it a bit, bullets were whizzing around like angry bees. I lay pretty flat in that sand dune over there, I can tell you."

"Did they kill anyone ?" asked John, rubbing soap into his hair.

"Yes. They got two drivers of those lorries, the third managed to bale out into the ditch. He was jolly lucky not to go up on a mine at the side of the road. The whole verge is riddled with the beastly things."

"I never turn off the road except where I can see some other vehicle has been there before," said John with a grin, towelling his face vigorously. "Gad ! It's grand to get a wash. You never wash, do you Walter ?"

"Occasionally. — Let's go off and have a bathe after tea. We're not wanted till seven, when the C.O. is holding a conference to put us in the picture. He's been away at Corps Headquarters all morning. I think the Army Commander has been giving his usual talk to the C.O's. I wonder what it is all about this time. More battles, I expect. Hope it won't be as bad as Alamein. I've had enough of that sort of show. Mobile warfare, that's what I want to see."

"My dear chap, what sort of warfare do you call this anyway ? Out all the way from Scotland, across about twenty thousand miles of ocean, and then chasing the Bosche half-way across Africa into the bargain. If that isn't mobile warfare, I'd like to know what is."

"I know all that. It's these set-piece battles with a terrific barrage all laid on that I don't like. I'd rather do a bit of stalking like you used to hear about in the Boer War. That must have been fun. I wonder if we'll ever do anything like that."

"We might, if only we could get the beggars on the run out of this Wadi Chebir position. Are you off to tea?"

"Yes, I think so. I feel like a cup, my mouth is as dry as a bucket of sand."

"Hold on a moment and I'll come along with you."

John hastily finished his toilet and they walked away to the Officers Mess. Later on, after they had had their bathe in the sea, they attended a conference held by the C.O. in a little hollow in the sand dunes, by the light of the brilliant full moon. All the officers in the battalion were there, and the C.O. gave them the picture of the projected operation. On the ground was a scale model of the country over which they were to operate, and the officers had grouped themselves around it. The C.O. was standing with a long stick in his hand which he used as a pointer.

"Now, Gentlemen," he said. "There isn't much time, and I've a lot to get through. So will you all please listen hard. I'll run through the business and we'll have questions at the end."

He used the pointer to indicate places on the model, clearly visible in the bright moonlight.

"This Wadi here is the Wadi Chebir. The one further West is the Wadi Mrah. Further on is the Wadi Uesca, and beyond this the Wadi Chieff. The deep depression away to the North West is the Wadi Zem Zem, where the Bosche has dug himself in. Facing him, our own forward infantry are patrolling into the Wadi Chieff, but up till now we haven't got much definite information as to his gun positions. We have managed to pin-point several machine-gun emplacements. Here they are."

"Now for the show. In a few days time we are going forward to take up our positions opposite the enemy here. The New Zealanders will be away out on the left flank, as usual, doing their famous left hook. There will be an armoured formation between them and ourselves, but we shall be the only infantry division in the battle. Our job is to follow up the coast road as fast as we can, and try to get to Tripoli before the armour who are going to treck right across the desert. The road is certain to be mined, so we shall have to move about two miles inland from it. The Sappers are going to have a tough job debunking the mines all the way up, but we won't have time to wait for them, so we shall just push on as quickly as we can."

"The day after to-morrow, we move from here up to the Wadi Uesca, and take over from the Brigade holding the line at the present time. We won't have much time to study the ground, so I want all of you to memorise this model. As most of you know already, the maps are rather indifferent in this part of the world, so don't you trust them too much."

"If I were you, I'd make a sketch of this model. You'll find it far more accurate than any of the maps you have been issued with. The Wadi Chieff is about two thousand yards wrong on our maps, don't them at all, if you can help it."

"When the time comes for us to advance, we shall do so on a two company front. You, Bill, will be on the right, as usual, and "B" Company on the left.

Battalion Headquarters will follow "A" Company, being the one nearest to the road. There will be the usual barrage, just as we had at Alamein, but I don't expect that the enemy will have anything like the number of guns firing that he had on that occasion. I hope he won't, anyway. We've got the detailed reports of all patrols for the last ten days, and I want you all to study them in detail when you get them. The Adjutant is sending them round to companies to-morrow."

"Get your maps marked up with all located enemy machine-gun positions, and see that you know where their wire lies. The methods will be exactly the same as they were for Alamein. There will be Sapper mine-lifting parties who are to report to us on the evening of the attack. There will be Bofors guns firing at intervals to show us the direction if we get lost, as they did the last time. You should all know the drill by now, but I want you to make certain that every one of your men knows exactly what his objective is, and who is to be on each side of him throughout the operation. You know my methods, or at least you jolly well ought to. Every man jack in this battalion is to be entirely in the picture from the start, so that he can do the right thing even if his immediate leaders are knocked out."

The Colonel went on to deal with every little detail of the coming attack, and by the time he had finished, every officer knew and understood what was expected of him.

In the old days, soldiers were never told anything of the Higher Commander's plan. Surely this was the greatest mistake. How can a soldier be expected to do the right thing when his officer has been killed, unless he knows exactly what the whole thing is about? If he knows and understands the object of the operation and the part to be played by his particular unit, he is far more likely to make a success of it than if he is left completely in the dark, to act as an automaton? Throughout the Eighth Army, the same principle held good during the whole campaign. Every man in the ranks was sent into battle with a full knowledge of what was going on, and what was at stake. There was no muddle thinking and leaving of things to chance. If a junior leader became a casualty, the next senior soldier on the spot was well able to take charge. The system was a good one, and it worked. Soldiers are not robots. They appreciate being put into the big picture, and they pay a handsome dividend if they are treated the right way.

Two days passed in hectic preparation, and then the Inverness Regiment moved to take up their positions in the Wadi Uesca. It was a dreary journey in their lorries. The country was flat and uninteresting in the extreme, being composed of shallow wadis separated by wide stretches of hard, rocky soil, far too hard to dig.

It was getting dusk as they approached the Wadi Uesca. It would have been impossible to motor so far forward in the full light of day without being observed by the enemy. Even so they were set upon by some six prowling Messerschmitts, which, however, must have run out of ammunition after the opening shots, for they soon left them alone and flew back to their aerodrome in the West. Nobody was hurt, and the long column continued its way into the dusk of the desert.

They stopped short of the Wadi Uesca, and John Gray found himself leading his platoon over some of the hardest ground he had ever imagined. They met guides who led them to their correct localities. Without these guides it would have been almost impossible to find the right place, every wadi and hillock looked exactly the same, and the map was very little use.

John eventually sited his platoon on the reverse slopes of a small hill a little way beyond the Western outlets of the Wadi Uesca. The ground was a little softer here, and they were able to dig a reasonable number of slit trenches in the ground. He put out his sentries and arranged for patrols to be sent out. Then he got down to it for the rest of the night. There was no object in remaining awake. On the morrow there was an attack coming off, and every minute's sleep was precious.

CHAPTER XIII

THE BATTLE OF THE WADI ZEM ZEM

THE SIGNALS COLONEL WASN'T FEELING ANY TOO happy when he arrived at Battle Headquarters of the Division. It was still early in the day, and he was setting out with the GOC to see where everybody was going to be for the advance late that night. It was not at all like the battle of Alamein, where he had had a good three weeks to lay his multitude of field telephone cables, and to bury them well under the earth. This time it was a rush to be ready at the last minute. There was no object in laying his wire out days beforehand, since the ground was far too hard to consider burying any lines.

The great problem was to find out where the various battalions and Artillery Regiments were going to be located, and to get them linked up with telephone cables in time for the show that night. Then, of course, in all probability, most of these cables, laid down on the bare surface of the ground, would be cut by the advancing tanks. The Colonel wished that the whole business was successfully over and done with. However, he followed the GOC all round the front, and when he returned to Headquarters he had a fairly clear picture of the position.

This all sounds very vague, but those who have been in that part of the Western Desert will know how impossibly inaccurate the maps were. There were, in fact, many arguments as to the exact position of even big features of the landscape, and you never could be certain if you were standing in any particular Wadi.

The country was uninteresting in the extreme. There were a few parallel wadis, so shallow as to be hardly worthy of the name. They were merely shallow, little valleys cut into the eternal flatness of the landscape, although, between the Wadi Uesca and the Wadi Zem Zem the country was of a gently undulating nature, interspersed with very shallow depressions in which a few vehicles could lie comparatively well hidden from observation. Of cover from the air there was none. Between these small valleys, the ground was hard and stony. When you went out for a run in a Jeep, you felt for all the world like a fly on the tight surface of a drum. If you were unlucky, and a couple of German fighter planes discovered you, there was nothing else to do but to leap out of your Jeep, run a few yards away and lie down, hoping that they would go for the vehicle and leave you alone.

The Signals Colonel held a conference on his return from the reconnaissance with the GOC. He gave out orders as to what lines were to be laid, and what wireless sets and crews were to serve the different headquarters. Then he went to see Captain Alec Foster, who was superintending the installation of telephones and exchanges for the use of the Staff during the coming battle.

"Hullo, Sir," said Foster, as the Colonel approached. "We're getting on fine with this job. Care to have a look inside?"

"Yes, Alec, I will," said the Colonel, clambering down into the shallow scrape which had been dug in the hard ground of the little wadi.

"I don't think there's any object in trying to get this place any deeper," said Foster, "it's only a waste of time. Unless we could get it six feet under ground, it's just as safe as it is now. There wouldn't anyway be the time left to do it now even if we wanted to."

"I quite agree, Alec, but you'd better get an alternative place prepared a couple of hundred yards away, in case you get a direct hit here during the show. You remember young Douglas getting a shell right in the middle of his Signal Office in the Alamein show? We can't risk that happening here, and not being ready for it. So I think you'd better have a small telephone exchange set up over there with the really vital lines all laid on to it, just in case of accidents."

"I think you're right, Sir, I'll get it done later on in the afternoon. I must get this finished first, and then I'll put Sergeant Macintosh and his boys to prepare the alternative place. How will that suit you, Sir?"

"That will do fine, Alec."

They went on discussing spares and wireless details, and then the Colonel decided to go and visit two of the infantry brigades, to see that they had all they needed for the night's battle. His worries were largely worries of equipment, and it was up to him to see that none of his units lacked anything.

The attack was due to start at eleven at night, and at half past ten, there was the distinct rumble of tanks moving up through the Divisional reserve position. A few odd shells were bursting every now and then on the ridge forward of Divisional Headquarters, but nobody paid much attention to them; all were far too busy to heed the explosion of a few stray shells.

At nine o'clock, every one of the telephone cables had been reported 'through', and the Signals men had felt thoroughly satisfied with their part of the business. The Colonel was sitting outside the Signal Office talking to Major Carter, when an orderly came up and reported the line out of order to one of the Brigades. A few moments after, Douglas Macdonald, who was in charge of the Office, put his head out and remarked that another of their lines had gone down. Within five minutes, every single one of their carefully laid telephone cables was reported out of order.

"Blast those tanks!" exclaimed the Colonel. "I was afraid this would happen. We may have to rely on wireless, James," he remarked to Major Carter, getting to his feet. "But we must get every available man out to put the lines through again as quickly as we can."

"Every man I can spare is out already, Sir," said young Macdonald, his face worried with anxiety. "I haven't got any more. What shall I do, Sir?"

The Colonel thought for a minute. "I know what, James. We'll wait till these tanks have passed through, and then you and I and any other officers or drivers we can get hold of will go out and put these beastly lines through again. Come on, let's see who we can find."

A party of nine men and three officers were eventually gathered together, and after the tanks had rumbled past on their way forward, this little band of scratch linemen sallied forth to see what they could do. The Colonel and Major Carter went with them, there was work for each one, and to spare.

The result was that at half past eleven, after the barrage had been going for half an hour, every field telephone cable had been mended, and those directing the battle were once again able to talk to each other and exchange orders and information. But it had been a nasty time for the Signals Colonel. He was responsible for the good working of the telephone system, and it had been a rude shock to know that a battalion of tanks had torn all his lines to shreds in many places, just when an attack was about to start. It was only after herculean efforts on the part of this little scratch party that order was eventually produced out of chaos. It had been touch and go, but the task had been done in an incredibly short time. For the rest of the night, the lines held except for an occasional break which was soon located and repaired, and news of how the attack was progressing came filtering back to the people who awaited it.

* * *

Lieutenant John Gray sat waiting in a little wadi with his platoon. It was fifteen minutes to eleven, and the barrage was due to open at the clock hour.

His company was once again in the right lead, with 'B' Company on their left. All looked much the same as it had done in the Alamein battle, save that the country was far flatter and much more rocky. They had been unable to dig in the hard ground. The men were lying down at the bottom of the little valley in which their Company was resting before the march to their Start Line.

John was getting used to battles. He realised exactly what he was in for, and had no silly ideas as to what walking behind a barrage entailed for himself and his men. There was nothing you could do about it, you just walked on till you came to the wire and trusted to luck that you wouldn't step on an enemy mine, or be hit by one of the many shells that came swishing over on top of the attackers. Every officer and sergeant had had the opportunity of studying aerial photographs of the enemy position in front of them, and they knew where each platoon was expected to go. They would be able to recognise the place when they arrived there, and which of the enemy machine-gun posts they were to attack, if they got the chance. It was no use taking any notice of the bullets and shells that came on top of you, as you could never hope to avoid your particular one, if by ill luck it happened to have your name on it. You just hoped for the best, there was nothing else to be done.

"Ready, old boy?" Major Wilson spoke. He had come up silently behind John Gray as he sat on the ground musing.

"All ready, Sir. How long have we got now?"

Major Wilson glanced at his watch. "I make it six minutes to the hour," he said. "We ought to get ready to move. I want to start from here sharp on the stroke of eleven. That'll take us across the Start Line at ten minutes past, and we must not be late. Come on, get your chaps ready."

"Right you are, Sir," said John beckoning to his Sergeant. A few moments later, the whole Company was on the move, twisting about the desert in the darkness, like a series of silent snakes. There was a full moon, and it was possible to see for quite a distance. All at once, the artillery barrage opened up. They had been expecting it, but it was none the less awe-inspiring when it started. There was a shattering crash of guns behind them, followed by the usual flickering lights on the far horizon, where the shells were bursting in hundreds. From right to left and back again, like a firework display, the fearful flashes danced before the eyes of the advancing infantry. There were hardly any shells coming back from the enemy's side, but a few big ones fell fairly near to the advancing Inverness Regiment. Nobody was hurt, however.

They had gone a full mile before they had their first casualty. Unexpectedly, a German machine-gun opened up on them from away to their right front. Bullets swished past them, and John ducked down instinctively. There was a scream from just behind him, and his runner fell to the ground, writhing. John dropped back to have a look at him, but the lad was dead before he reached him. He turned him over, and hurriedly turned him back again on his face, shuddering with horror. Some wounds are best not seen by those who have not yet been hit. The whole of the boy's chest had been shattered. It was not at all a nice sight.

Feeling very sick, John hurried back to his place in the lead. The machine-gun was still firing, but not at them any more. They carried on unmolested till they came to the first enemy minefield, where a party of Sappers were hard at it clearing pathways through the mines. The dark shapes of several men on the ground in the middle of the minefield told John how risky a job it was to remove enemy mines under fire. There was a pause until the first of the gaps was ready, then they passed through in single file, without any untoward incident. As they emerged into the open again at the other side of the minefield, two men at the back of John's platoon fell to the earth, screaming with pain. There was no time to go back to see what could be done for them. The medical orderlies would soon be along to give them aid. — This was one of the worst parts of battle, John thought. Even if your own brother was hit, you had no right to stop behind to give him a hand. All you could do was to carry on marching forward and hope that you wouldn't be the next one to catch it.

Beyond the first minefield they came upon several disused dugouts, but even after a thorough search, there was no enemy to be found in them. So John and his platoon continued the advance across this desolate stretch of desert, which was for all the world like a huge, lost sea somewhere on the moon. Away to his left, John could hear the strains of the pipes coming from the Company piper who always marched immediately behind Major Wilson. He looked across, but to his horror he couldn't see the Major in his usual place. The piper was there all right, but no sign of the Major. Then he saw the Company Sergeant Major running across the sands in his direction, and he guessed what he was about to be told. Being the senior platoon officer, he would have to take command of the Company in the event of the Major becoming a casualty.

"Will you come across, Sir?" said the Sergeant Major, saluting smartly. "The Major's been hit and we've had to leave him."

"Is he badly hit?" asked John anxiously, for he had been very fond of Major Wilson.

"Only in the leg, Sir, but I fear he won't be able to walk again for a long time. The left leg is broken below the knee. Will you please come over and command the Company?"

"I'll be right over," replied John. "Sergeant Jackson!"

"Here, Sir," replied the sergeant at his elbow.

"Take over the platoon, will you. The Major's been hit and I have to go and command the company."

"Don't you worry about the platoon, Sir. I'll look after them all right."

"I'm sure you will, Jackson. Good luck to you."

"And good luck to you, Sir."

John went off with the Sergeant Major to the place where his Major had been accustomed to walk.

"Send a runner back to Battalion to say that I've taken over 'A' Company," he said to the Sergeant Major.

"I've already done so, Sir."

"Good man. Then we'll push on."

Battle is like that. You never can tell when the call will come. Either you get hit and are out of it for good, if you are lucky; or your superior gets hit and you find yourself with far more responsibility than you had a few short minutes before. Young John Gray was not afraid of the responsibility, he had forseen such an eventuality and had prepared himself to command a company at any moment. But it was nevertheless a bit of a thrill to find himself in this position in the very middle of a battle like this. He glanced about him to make sure that he knew where the other two platoons were, and waved to their commanders to show them that he was at the helm. Both young officers gave answering waves, and he could just make out their grins of encouragement in the moonlight. He squared his shoulders and set himself to the task in hand.

A little way further on, shells started to fall thick and fast into the ranks of the Inverness Regiment. They had reached the area into which the Germans were dropping their artillery defensive fire. But they continued to advance steadily to the incessant drone of the pipes played by the stalwart little figure striding out so bravely a few paces ahead of John Gray.

A few men fell, either killed or wounded, in the ranks of the two leading platoons, but for the most part, the Regiment continued to advance steadily without much loss. The Gunners behind them were doing all they knew to maintain the creeping barrage just a hundred yards or so in front of the leading infantry. Young John Gray kept urging his men to keep well up with the barrage, knowing from bitter experience that it is far safer to risk a few casualties in keeping close behind your own guns, than to hang too far back and allow the enemy time to pop up again after the barrage has passed by, and before you reach him.

There was one more minefield to cross, this time without the guidance of any friendly Sappers to point out the presence of the deadly mines. On they went, stepping warily, lest they should tread on an 'S' mine and be blown into little pieces. One of the sergeants, walking less than twenty yards behind John, was unlucky. He must have stepped right on top of one of these infernal machines, for there was a violent explosion, and after the smoke had cleared away, there was the wretched man lying on the ground in a pool of blood, his left leg hanging by a mere shred of skin. Luckily for him, two stretcher bearers were following close behind, and they managed to improvise a field dressing on the spot. The sergeant lived to tell the tale, but he had to lose his leg, and passed out of the war for good and all.

At the other side of the minefield, John caught sight of dim shapes of humanity looming out of the night some fifty yards ahead.

"Come on lads!" he shouted. "In we go with the bayonet!"

There was a concentrated rush of soldiers wielding glistening bayonets on the muzzles of their rifles, and ferocious howls and cheers as the Jocks ran helter skelter after those dim figures of the enemy. It takes time to tell, but in actual fact it was all over in about one minute. But for that minute, the men of the Inverness Regiment outdid themselves. They lunged and they struck, impaling terrified Germans and Italians on the points of their bayonets. It seemed to young John Gray that Hell itself had broken loose on earth. The night air was rendered hideous with the screams of the wounded and the dying. No quarter was asked for or given, and both sides fought with the grim determination of mad-men.

Then, all of a sudden, the enemy broke and started to fly from the position. One moment they were there, a mass of struggling humanity, the next, they were running for their lives, leaving their dead and wounded on the field, and the men of the Inverness Regiment in undisputed possession of the position.

"Come on, Lads. Get dug in!" urged John Gray, remembering the teachings of Major Wilson. "They'll counter-attack us as sure as my name's Gray. Sergeant Major! Tell No.1 Platoon to dig in here, No.2 over there in that wadi, No.3 here on my left. We'll have a mortar down in that little hollow, and Company Headquarters will be right here. Understand?"

"Quite clear, Sir," replied the Sergeant Major, thanking his stars that this young officer was taking a grip on the proceedings. He hurried off to carry out his orders.

"How are things, young man?"

John turned round and saw Colonel Forsyth standing beside him.

"Quite under control, Sir," replied John, saluting smartly. "Major Wilson was hit, so I am carrying on."

"And doing very well indeed, John," went on the Colonel, patting him on the shoulder. He glanced about him. "Show me your positions."

John quickly pointed out how he had disposed his Company, and the Colonel expressed his approval.

"Well done, youngster," he said. "But get your chaps well dug in before light. It's ten to one they'll try to counter-attack before dawn. So you'd better be ready for it. I'm asking the Gunners to put down defensive fire bang in front of here, if we put up the normal SOS signal. — Well, I must be off. You sit tight here. Goodbye."

The Colonel departed to see the Company on their left, and John hastened to superintend the digging-in of his position. He walked from Section to Section, urging the men to work like beavers to get themselves well below ground. By daylight, they were in a very strong position indeed, capable of withstanding any attack the Germans might attempt to launch.

Dawn came at last, but still no attack. There were no shells coming over, and no small-arms fire. John eventually sent out a patrol. They returned to report that they could find no trace of the enemy. The

Germans had made use of the last hours of darkness to slip away across the Wadi Zem Zem and off Northwards in the general direction of Misurata and Tripoli.

The men of the Inverness Regiment had had another victory, but they well knew that this was just a phase in the general advance of the Eighth Army. Their objective was still Tripoli, and it would not be long before they were continuing the advance. News came in during the morning of the success of the armoured formations on their left. By noon, another battalion passed through their position, and the Inverness Regiment reverted for the time being into Brigade Reserve.

CHAPTER XIV

AMBUSH

COLONEL DENMAN WAS IN HIGH SPIRITS. THINGS had gone well during the attack of the previous night, and all the signal cables had held for the time they had been required. The attack had been successful, and now that morning had come, the reserve Brigade had passed through and was hard at work pursuing the fast retreating enemy in the direction of Misurata. A few of the Signals officers were sitting in the shade of the Mess lorry, eating their breakfast and comparing notes about the night before.

"That's the first time for many a long year that I have been out on a line myself, James," the Colonel said to Major Carter, with a broad smile.

"Me too, Sir," grinned Carter, helping himself to more biscuits and jam. There was no marmalade to be had up there in the desert, and they had almost forgotten what it tasted like.

"When are we moving on, Sir ?" asked Alec Foster.

"Within the next hour or so, as far as I can tell. I'll let you know as soon as I've seen the G1, but I expect you'll be off almost any time now."

"Are you coming with me, Sir ?"

"No, not this time. I'm not much use back here now. I've a feeling that we won't stop again before we get to Misurata. I'll slip on ahead and find out what is going on and perhaps I'll be able to tell you something about it when you make up on me. We've reached the stage of the 'Fog of War' you know, Alec."

"I suppose we have, Sir. But don't you go getting yourself taken prisoner, or doing anything foolish like that. We don't want to lose you at this stage of the proceedings. You might not have paid your Mess Bill, you know, Sir, and that wouldn't do at all, would it ?"

"Idiot," grinned the Colonel.

They finished their meal, and went their various ways to prepare for the move forward which was likely to take place during the morning. Foster was the first to leave, with his retinue of wireless sets and a cable detachment under the able command of John Craig. The Colonel stayed behind for a couple of hours to see to the organisation of the rest of the unit, then he got into his car and followed up after the Advance Party.

The track was very dusty, but well defined owing to the great number of vehicles which had already passed along it. It took him across a very flat stretch of desert, over which the Inverness Regiment had attacked the night before. The first two miles were uninteresting in the extreme, just flat plain with hardly any scrub or bushes to relieve the monotony. Overhead, there were several aeroplanes, flying pretty low. The Colonel stood up in his car to have a look at them. You never could tell when an enemy plane would swoop on top of you and come down blazing away with its machine-guns. He always kept the roof of the car open; by standing on the seat and sticking his head through the sliding roof he got a very good, all-round view of the heavens above. The planes streaked away to the North with half a dozen others in hot pursuit. They were obviously Germans with a squadron of Kittyhawks on their tails. The Colonel watched till they had faded out of sight in the morning haze, but did not see any of them shot down. That was the trouble with aerial battles, you so rarely saw the finish of any particular fight. The planes usually passed over you at an incredible speed and were lost to sight before anything interesting happened.

There were no anti-aircraft guns in action, owing to the presence of our own fighters. The guns always kept silent when our own planes put in an appearance, as they didn't want to shoot any of our own side down by mistake.

The troops passed through the gap in the minefield, a narrow lane between two stretches of barbed wire, marked by white tapes on either side of the pathway. Lorry after lorry, at an interval of about a hundred yards, a long stream of vehicles, the transport of the brigade, was moving up to the battle front, laden with troops in their shirt sleeves. The Highland Division was in hot pursuit of the fast retreating enemy.

The Colonel pulled out of the column as soon as his car had passed through the gap. By edging off the track, he was able to overtake the moving column, though to do so was rather a risky business, as there might well be laid hidden mines at the sides of the track. But he was lucky, and nothing happened to him all the way up the line. One of his lorries following after with the main body wasn't so lucky. It hit a mine right in the middle of the track, where you would never have expected any mines to be. None of the men were injured, but the lorry was a complete write-off.

A few miles further on, he overtook the leading lorry of this Brigade, and had a clear stretch of country ahead of him. They passed outside the village of Gheddadia and made their way on simply by following the tracks of those who had passed that way before. It would have been suicidal to follow the coast road, as that had been well and truly mined by the enemy before he decided to retreat. The Sappers were hard at work removing the mines, but it would be several days before it was safe to drive a vehicle along it, and so the whole Division was moving up a track which they had marked out for themselves some two miles inland from the coast road. This was far safer, and reasonably clear of mines.

It was a pleasant day's run. Their track led them through fairly green country, studded with small bushes, a relief from the eternal sands which they had for so long been accustomed to. Except for an occasional blur on the horizon on either side, there were very few vehicles to be seen, and the Colonel wondered if he were following the right track after all. Still, they were going steadily Northward, so they couldn't be very much wrong. They followed throughout the day the never-ending tracks across the rugged plain towards a horizon which never seemed to come any nearer.

Towards evening, they came to a small hill in the middle of the plain, and saw shell bursts two miles away.

"Looks as though we were getting nearer the War, Booth," said the Colonel to his driver with a smile.

"We'll be seeing TAC Headquarters before long, I think, Sir," said the man, quite unmoved. Shell fire never worried the imperturbable Booth. He was a mechanical engineer from Aberdeen, and had hoped to settle down in South Africa before the war upset all his plans.

After a little searching they came across Alec Foster and his gang of Signal lads, preparing for the next move forward.

"How are things, Alec?"

"First Class, Sir. It really looks as if we had the beggars on the run this time. We are due to leave this place in an hour's time from now. The Brigade in front are moving now, and they expect to be in Misurata before daylight to-morrow. I think the General's going off to the Corps Commander soon, so you'd better see him now, Sir."

"Where is he, Alec?"

"Over there, in his caravan," and Foster pointed in the direction of a large vehicle just visible in the gathering twilight.

"I'll go across, and have a word with you later on," said the Colonel moving off towards the GOC's caravan

He found the General in high spirits, and just about to leave to see the Corps Commander. The rest of the Battle Headquarters were to move on towards Misurata in a few minutes, and the GOC would rejoin them there after his visit to Corps.

The Colonel had a few words with the G1 who was in charge of the move. It was decided that the G1 would lead, followed by the office lorries and wireless trucks, the Signals Colonel bringing up the rear. He would thus be in a position to know if any of his precious wireless vehicles or cable lorries fell by the wayside during the long march. They had about eighty miles to go, and it would not at all be easy to recognise the track in the darkness, even though there was a fairly good moon to light them on their way.

They started off in single file of vehicles. The cloud of dust stirred up by the little convoy was so dense, that it was almost impossible to see even as far as the car ahead. Hour after hour they travelled through the night, only stopping once to make a check on their position. It was for all the world like steering a convoy of ships across the uncharted seas. The tracks were very ill defined, and they had continually to stop and restart as a vehicle here and there got stuck in the soft sand. As the night wore on, the Colonel got more and more sleepy and finally dozed off into a fitfull sleep. It was half past two in the morning when he was wakened up suddenly by a shape out of the darkness which opened the door of his car and grabbed hold of his arm.

"Are you an officer, Sir?" asked a strange voice.

The Colonel peered out into the open air, half fuddled

with sleep. He made out the figure of a man dressed as a Major, wearing a steel helmet on his head, and looking like a lost sheep.

"What's up?" asked the Colonel in a sleepy voice.

"I'm the Political Officer with the column supposed to be going into this town," said the man outside. "We've been ambushed about six miles farther on up the track, and there are a lot of men killed. The Colonel has had both his legs shot off, and there aren't any officers left. I don't know exactly what to do, and there are men I want to get off in an ambulance, if I could tell where to find one."

Colonel Denman got out of his car and looked about him. There were only about ten vehicles round about. Where had the rest got to?

"Do you know where we are?" he asked the Political Officer.

"Yes, about seven miles South of Misurata, and five from Crispi. Our column was driving through Crispi when we were shot up. There must have still been Germans in the place. They beat us up badly, and no mistake. But look, Sir. There are wounded men to see to, and I must do something about it. What would you advise I should do?"

"Let's have a look at what we have here," said the Colonel, walking along the line of vehicles to see which were left. There were a few clerk's lorries, two cable detachments, and the Headquarters of the Divisional Sappers. That was all; of the G1 and the rest of the Battle Headquarters there was no sign. It was easy to see what had happened. One of the vehicles in the centre of the convoy must have stopped in the middle of the night, unknown to those in front. The front half of the convoy had driven on, leaving the other half behind. This was the other half which the Colonel found himself left with. And there were no fighting soldiers in the whole bunch. Just a few clerks and a party of linemen, that was all. This was no army with which to set forth to straighten up any such nasty thing as an ambush in which a good many men had been killed already.

The Colonel soon made up his mind. He ordered the vehicles to be formed up into a square, and placed sentries at each of the four corners. He decided to go ahead by himself to find out what had happened, and to see if it were now safe for the rest of them to proceed. He wasn't very keen to do so, it smelt like an unpleasant business, but he felt that he had no option in the matter. He couldn't very well detail any of the other officers for such a sticky task, so he had naturally to go himself.

"You all stop here," he said. "I'm going on ahead to see what there is to be seen."

"I'm coming with you, Sir," said John Craig, the Cable Section Officer.

"No, you're not, John," said the Colonel, very firmly.

"I beg your pardon, Sir," replied John Craig, speaking very low and in a determined voice. "But I can't let you go off alone on a show like this, all by yourself. So, if you don't mind, I'm coming along with you."

The Colonel inwardly heaved a sigh of relief. He certainly would be glad to have the youngster's company, it would be no fun at all creeping about on his stomach in the sand, looking for the enemy who would certainly still be there.

"All right, young man," he laughed. "You win. Come on, we'll take this Armoured Reconnaissance Car from the Sappers. I'm sure they won't mind; will you let us, Bill ?" and he turned to the Sapper Adjutant who was listening to their conversation.

"Take it with pleasure, Sir. But be careful not to get written off. We don't want to lose you yet awhile."

"I'll be very careful, don't you worry about that," remarked the Colonel, as he and John Craig climbed into the vehicle. They closed the slits in the windscreen and felt a little more protected. Then they started off in the direction of Crispi and Misurata, following the tracks of previous vehicles. A whole Brigade had passed along that way, but they had kept to the left of the track, leaving the stretch of country between it and the sea completely untouched. It must have been in this stretch that the Germans had lain in wait for the little column of Colonial Troops which were supposed to go into Crispi and take the place over. The sea was only a bare two miles away to the East, but the visibility was not more than fifty yards.

They proceeded slowly for about three miles, and then something loomed up in the darkness ahead. The Colonel told the driver to pull off to the left and stop. Motioning John Craig to remain with the car, he jumped out and walked swiftly away to the right to see what the approaching shape could be. Peering through the darkness, he saw that it was a vehicle, and after a few moments, it turned out to be an ambulance, driving very slowly up one of the tracks which ran parallel to the one he had just left. It seemed pretty certain that this ambulance would hold some of the troops who had been shot up, and most unlikely that it could belong to the enemy, or it would surely be driving in the opposite direction.

The Colonel had removed his coat before he started and taken off his revolver belt, carrying the weapon in his trouser pocket. This had lightened his load so that he would be able to run like a rabbit if the occasion demanded it. He sprinted across the sand after the ambulance, and managed to make up on it before it had gone too far. The driver saw the officer coming, and brought his vehicle to a standstill.

"Who are you?" asked the Colonel, slightly out of breath from his brisk run.

"Freddy Field Ambulance, Sir," replied the driver. "I've got a load of wounded black men in the back. I picked them up about a mile further on down this track."

"Do you know what happened?"

"Not much, Sir. But I understand that they got ambushed near Crispi. Two of their own vehicles brought them back to a small house on the right hand side a little way farther on from here. There is an officer down there, Sir. I think you'd better go on and talk to him about it. I must get on with these chaps, some of them are pretty bad."

"Yes, you go on," said the Colonel. "I'll go forward and try to find out what has happened."

The ambulance started off slowly once more, and was soon swallowed up in the darkness. The Colonel made his way back to the Armoured car and told John Craig what he had seen and heard.

"So it's true enough about the ambush, Sir," remarked John.

"Looks rather like it, John," answered the Colonel, and told the driver to get back once more on their track, and to follow it.

A mile farther on they came to the small house the driver of the ambulance had spoken about. Sure enough, there was a party of men gathered in front of it, and among them several officers of the Division. The Colonel spoke to one of them who turned out to be the Adjutant of one of the battalions of the Brigade which had gone ahead earlier in the night. Like the Colonel, he had got left behind with his party, and was trying to re-join his unit. He had run into this group of wounded Colonial troops, and had been trying to elucidate what had happened when the Colonel arrived on the scene.

"Do you know where the enemy are now?" asked the Colonel.

"Haven't the foggiest idea, Sir. But I gather that these johnnies were fired on just as they started to enter the town of Crispi. There must have been a couple of machine-guns and perhaps an anti-tank gun, as they had five of their vehicles knocked out. Their Colonel is in that ambulance over there, and the doctor says he won't live very long. He has had both legs shot off, and is in a very bad way indeed."

"What rotten luck! — I wonder how it all happened," murmured the Colonel. "Have you been any further on from here?"

"Not yet, Sir. But I think I'll go along now. I don't want to get mixed up in this show, as I've to join my battalion as quickly as I can. They'll be wondering what has happened to me."

"Well, you keep to the left of the main track and you, ought to be all right," said the Colonel. "It seems to me that the trouble was all well East of that track. They were probably driving light-heartedly into Crispi without bothering to send out scouts ahead to have a look-see before they entered the place. It's always that way. If you don't take reasonable precautions, you get let down in the long run."

"Too true, Sir. I'll take your advice and stick to the left hand side of the track. Are you coming along, Sir?"

"No, I don't think I will. I'll go on ahead on the right hand side and try to find out if the Germans are really there or not. I expect they've cleared out of it long ago. They could hardly remain there for long, after they realised that your Brigade was getting behind their rear."

"We'll, I'll be off, Sir. Good-night to you."

"Good-night."

The officer went off in his Jeep, the Colonel to the Armoured Car where he had left young John Craig with the driver.

"What's to do, Sir?" asked John.

"It's quite true. There has been a nasty little show in Crispi. A good many of the black men have been killed or wounded, and their Colonel has lost both legs above the knee. He's in an ambulance over there, but they don't think he'll live till the morning."

"Was that the Colonel who had dinner with us the night before last, Sir?"

"That's the fellow. He was a pretty decent chap, and I'm sorry about it."

"So am I, Sir. What rotten luck!"

"That may be so, John my lad, but we've got to push on and find out whether it's safe for our own little convoy to proceed. I don't relish the idea of being a Boy Scout, and creeping about on my tummy looking for Germans in this part of the world, but I'm afraid we've got to do something about it. After all, we do know that there has been a party of Bosche in these parts, and that some troops have been shot up going into Crispi, and I'm certainly not risking taking my own chaps there until I'm sure that the Bosche have left."

They drove on for about two miles, then the white roof-tops of the little village of Crispi became clearly visible in the bright moonlight. There had been a lot of clouds when they set out but these had now cleared away, and they were able to see pretty distinctly.

"Let's stop and listen if we can hear anything," said the Colonel at length, and the driver pulled the car up to a standstill. They switched off the engine and got out of the vehicle. For a few moments they stood there listening intently, then John Craig thought he heard something.

"Do you hear a lorry moving along that track, Sir?" he asked.

"Where?"

"Over underneath the Pole Star." John pointed across the sand in the direction of the village, which must have been a good mile away.

The Colonel cupped his hands behind his ears and listened. The youngster's keen ears had been correct. There was the distinct sound of an engine drawing gradually nearer to them. Would it prove to be friend or foe? It was quite impossible to say without actually seeing the vehicle.

"You take the car over there, well to the left, John," said the Colonel. "Turn her round in case you have to make a quick get-away. I'll go off to the right and lie up in the sand dunes. Perhaps they'll pass close enough for me to see who they belong to. Hurry now, there isn't any time to be lost. They'll be level with us in a brace of shakes."

"For goodness sake be careful, Sir," said John anxiously. He didn't like the idea of the Colonel going off on his own.

"I'll be all right, old son," grinned the Colonel "But you are to do a bunk and run back and tell the others if I get shot up. There must be no coming along after me, mind."

"Right you are, Sir. But don't be away too long."

"I'll be right back, never fear." He melted away into the night in the direction of the approaching lorry. Running swiftly to get as far away from his own car as possible, he dodged about among the sand hills till he found a convenient high spot where he could observe without being seen.

The approaching lorry was now plainly visible in the moonlight. But it was impossible to see which side it belonged to, and even if it had been, that wouldn't have helped much. Both sides were in the habit of using captured vehicles for their own uses. Suddenly, the moving lorry stopped and turned round. With a little catch in his breath, the Colonel noted the big, solid wheels used by the Germans on their heavy lorries. This wasn't too good, and hardly pointing to it being one of the vehicles of the leading Brigade.

He kept on watching closely, and saw several figures get out of the lorry and cluster round in a little group. He could hear their voices quite plainly, but could not make out what language they were speaking. They were carrying arms, and several times the watcher heard a breech-bolt click. He felt that he must find out whether they were Germans or not. He left his vantage point and wormed his way on his stomach in the direction of the little group of men beside the vehicle. He got to within about thirty yards of them, when he heard another lorry coming along the track. Lying quite still, hardly daring to breathe, he waited till this second lorry had drawn level with the first one. It stopped too and turned round, while another party of men got out.

He listened intently, but could not catch what they were saying. But their language was most certainly not English. It may have been German and it may have been Italian, he could not get close enough to make out.

Anyway, the Colonel felt that lying on the sand playing at Boy Scouts was not part of his work as O.C. of the Divisional Signals, and if he couldn't find out what nationality these fellows belonged to, it was time he got back to his own people. So, with infinite care, he wormed his way to where it was possible to stand up without being seen from those lorries, and to run back to the waiting armoured car. Young John Craig was eager to know what he had found out.

"Are they Germans, Sir?" he asked, as the Colonel came up.

"God knows, old son. They certainly aren't English. I'll stake my oath on that. But I couldn't get near enough to find out what language they were talking. What about you having a shot at it? Your hearing is probably a good deal better than mine."

"You wait here, Sir, and I'll be right back."

"Be careful, youngster. There's no object in your getting so close that you get taken prisoner, you know."

"I'll watch my step, Sir," laughed John, and disappeared into the sand hills at a fast run.

It seemed ages till the boy came back, and the Colonel was quite worried when at last he came running up.

"Quite definitely not English, Sir," he gasped, out of breath with running. "And I'd be almost ready to swear that it's German they're speaking."

"Well done, youngster. Then this is where we beat a hasty retreat according to plan. We'll get back to the others and stop there for the rest of the night. I don't think those chaps will come any further in our direction. They'll probably make a bolt for it before daylight. Come on, let's go."

They got into the car and started to move back to where they had left the others. But almost at once, the engine died out.

"Out of petrol," remarked the driver.

"Have you got any more with you?" asked the Colonel, anxiously. This was no place to run out of fuel, with a couple of German lorries and a pretty strong patrol, within four hundred yards.

"Yes, Sir. I've got a tin in the back," replied the man. They all clambered out once more to get at the tin. The driver fumbled away trying to open it, and it was quite three minutes before the operation was over. They all had visions of those Germans coming over the small rise in the ground and discovering their presence before they had finished filling the tank. It was the longest three minutes that any of them had ever lived through. But at last the job was completed, and the engine burst into life.

They lost no time in jumping in, and drove off.

"I didn't see any good in trying to get any closer, John," remarked the Colonel. "We're far more use to our side alive than dead, and this is hardly Signalling in the accepted meaning of the word."

John laughed and glanced backwards to see if they were being followed. Nothing was to be seen. They had got away with it.

"I'm all for avoiding getting captured, Sir," he said. "I've a lassie back in Glasgow who wouldn't like it if the Bosche got a hold of me."

"I don't think I'd relish being taken prisoner either, John."

They drove back at a steady pace to where they had left the rest of their little party. The Colonel explained what they had seen, and decided that the best thing to be done was to post sentries out at the four corners of their small leaguer, and to sleep till it was light. Then they could go on and make up on the others. It would be decidedly foolish to try to push on that night, especially as there had been one ambush already.

So they got down to it in their vehicles, and all was quiet for the rest of the night.

CHAPTER XV

HOMS — TRIPOLI

Late in the afternoon, the Inverness Regiment arrived at the outskirts of Misurata. Their Brigade, still in reserve, was to concentrate on the forward slopes of the hills overlooking the sea. John Gray selected a place for his Company on the outer edge of the area allocated to the Regiment. His advance party was already there, and the trucks were ordered off to their respective places as they arrived.

The Colonel had told him that they were likely to remain at least till that afternoon, so the men got immediately down to prepare a meal. It was perfectly delightful out there in the sunshine. All around them was the green grass of the coastal plain, a welcome change after the never-ending sands which they had been accustomed to for so long. They had come to the end of the Desert very suddenly. One moment they had been following the usual kind of sandy track, with nothing but rocks and scrub on all sides, then unexpectedly this had all changed, and they found themselves driving through green fields where the local Arabs were tending their goats and tilling the soil.

"Have you heard about the conference?" Walter Mitchell asked John Gray who was sitting beside his truck.

"What conference, Walter? I've heard of no conference in these parts."

"The C.O. is holding one in half an hour's time from now, over there by his car. I'm running round telling chaps about it."

"What's to do?"

"Can't say, but I expect it's about our next move. It would be too good to be true if we stayed in this paradise for long."

"I must say I wish we could just bed down here for a day or two," said John with a sigh. He had been up all night and was feeling very tired and sleepy.

"There's no rest for the wicked," laughed Walter, as he passed on to warn the others.

John got to his feet and walked round the Company to see how the mens' breakfasts were getting on. It was a long time since they had had time to cook a decent meal, and the preparations were going on apace. He left them and wandered across to the Colonel's car to the conference. Most of the other officers had arrived when he got there, and the rest came up a few minutes later. They all sat down in a circle round the C.O.

"Well, gentlemen," started the Colonel. "I fear we won't be staying long in this delectable spot, but don't forget that our object is still Tripoli, and we'll never get there at all if we sit on our hunkers here for the rest of the war."

"The enemy is doing his level best to delay us, and is blowing all the bridges on the coast road as fast as he can. At the moment he is holding a pretty strong position just on the far side of Homs, and we are going to move up near there this evening. When we shall have to attack, I don't yet know, but it will be within the next forty eight hours, that is certain."

"I want you to see that all your ammunition and water is replenished before we leave here, and we are to get two days' rations into the bargain. The Advance parties will be ready to leave early in the afternoon, I'll tell you the exact time after I have seen the Brigadier. Once you have got things ready for the move, I want you to see that every available man sleeps for as long as he possibly can. You never know when we'll get the chance again."

"See that you all get your maps marked up before you leave. The Adjutant has one pretty well up to date, and you can come in one at a time and do your own. That's about all I can tell you for just now. So off you go about your business."

The conference broke up, and the officers dispersed to their various jobs, thankful that they had got the chance of some rest and sleep. They had had a long march, and no sleep since before the battle of the previous night. It didn't take long to draw the ammunition and water from the various sources, and most of the men were able to lay in a private stock of water from the pipe in Crispi. They had not seen so much drinking water during the whole time they had been in the Desert. It is never looked upon as being a precious commodity in civilised countries, but these soldiers had been on a daily ration of less than a gallon for many weeks past. This had had to serve for all purposes, cooking, washing and drinking. And you don't get much to drink out of that sort of ration!

Within an hour, the ground was littered with the sleeping bodies of the Regiment, and only those who had a job to do were left awake.

Late in the afternoon, they got the word to move on, and in half an hour they were once more on their way, heading across the foothills in the direction of Zleiten and Homs. It was very rough going, just like driving a car across the moors of the Scottish Borders, but they made good progress, and arrived at the large oasis outside the village of Zleiten before dark. It was rather a wonderful sight for these desert-weary wanderers. There were hundreds of tall palm trees laden with dates, and many attractive little native houses, made of brick and mud, nestling in the undergrowth. Hosts of small children scurried here and there, trying to get the soldiers to exchange tea and sugar for eggs. Each child invariable held up two or three eggs in its little hands, hoping that it might be able to persuade some soldier to barter his precious tea for them. The Arabs were very partial to tea, and would never take anything else in exchange for the eggs so dear to the heart of the British soldier. It is rather interesting to note in passing that the tea situation got so accute as a result of this bartering for eggs, that it had to be stopped by the issuing of a general order on the subject. But it still went on, though not so openly as before. Rather like buying golf balls from the caddies at your country club!

The Regiment paused at this oasis till the early hours of the morning, when the Reconnaissance parties came back to report. The C.O. again called a conference and put every officer in the picture. They were to move up beyond Zleiten and on till they came nearly to Homs. Here they would find one battalion of the leading Brigade holding the enemy, while the other two had been slipped out to the right, preparing to creep round the enemy's flank, by the sea.

The Brigade of the Inverness Regiment were to put in an attack late that afternoon, and there would be very little time for all concerned to have a look at the ground. But they could count on pretty decent artillery support, and it was far more important to hit the Bosche before he had time to dig himself in properly, than to lose precious hours in preparations.

They spent a long time pouring over maps, and getting the lie of the land over which they would have to advance. There were many arrangements to be made, but these were all settled before they moved off.

Colonel Forsyth went on ahead with the Company Commanders, so that they should be able to take advantage of every hour of daylight, and start on their reconnaissances immediately after first light. John handed over the Company to the next senior platoon commander, and departed with the others.

Almost immediately after leaving the oasis, they struck the main road. It was one of the broad tarmac variety, just like any decent road at home. John felt it a great relief to be able to drive along this highway after months of steering an uncertain passage across the deep sands of the desert. It was a sheer joy to speed along between palm trees and little houses scattered all along the route. It was a picture of reasonable civilisation, such as they had not seen for many months, a sight for sore eyes. Nothing could seem farther from the war. It was all wrong that men should be killing each other in this earthly paradise.

Just short of Homs, the little convoy stopped, and the Colonel left his car to have a word with the Divisional Commander who had his Battle Headquarters on the side of the road, amongst the trees. After a few minutes, they moved on, but only for a mile or so. Then they turned off, and drove some little way across green fields, till they came near the Headquarters of the battalion which was in the line at that place.

They left their vehicles, and walked the rest of the way. The Battalion Headquarters was esconced in a small ditch. They spent the next hour discussing the dispositions of the troops in the line, and the known positions of the enemy. The rest of the battalion arrived about three in the morning, and moved into position a short way behind the unit which was already there. The idea was that the Inverness Regiment would pass through the other late in the following afternoon.

All went well, and John Gray managed to get a pretty good view of his own part of the front during the morning. There was a nasty two hours when the Germans shelled them pretty accurately with heavy field guns. Several men were hit, and quite a few killed. But his Company were lucky this time, they sustained no casualties at all.

The feature they were to attack that afternoon was for all the world like Edinburgh Castle. It was a fort standing on the very top of a large, conical hill, on the Western side of the town of Homs. A considerable number of the enemy was holding this admittedly strong position, but the Inverness Regiment hoped to be able to take it at the point of the bayonet. They were to have the support of all the available artillery in the Division.

Far away to the right were the Roman ruins of Leptis Magna. Beyond these, a small force was edging its way round to the sea, with the intention of cutting off the enemy's rear and forcing him either to retreat or surrender. The time fixed for the Inverness Regiment to attack was three in the afternoon. At two, they moved up into the line beside the battalion already there. There was a good deal of spasmodic shelling, but nothing to worry about, and the move up went off without a hitch.

John's Company was to be on the right, once again, and their objective was the right hand edge of the old fort. Every man jack of them had been told what was the plan of attack.

It was a beautiful day, the sun shining brilliantly in a clear sky of tropical blue. The old fort stood out on top of the hill against the skyline. There must have been enemy observation posts up there, for every now and then shells came whistling over to burst accurately enough among the positions held by the

Inverness Regiment's Brigade. It was remarkable how few men were hit by these shells, although at times they fell thick and fast.

John Gray looked at his watch. It was five minutes to three. He was sitting beside a Company Commander of the battalion whose lines they were to pass through.

"You're just off, aren't you, Gray?" remarked the other officer.

"In a couple of minutes now," replied John, throwing away the end of his cigarette and adjusting his web belt.

"Good-luck, old boy. See you later on in Tripoli, I hope."

"Thanks, I hope so too. I've had enough of this sort of thing to last me for a long time. I hope we get a good few weeks' rest when we do reach the beastly place." They both laughed.

Suddenly the artillery opened up with every available gun, and the men around them started to walk steadily forward.

"So long!" shouted John to the other at his side. "Here we go." With that, he left the shelter of the ditch he had been crouching in and took his usual place at the head of his Company. The Sergeant Major was just behind him, as always, and his piper a few paces in front. A couple of hundred yards or so off to his right was No.1 Platoon, led by Hamish Macdonald, and the same distance to the left came No.2 Platoon, with No.3 about three hundred yards to the rear. 'B' Company was advancing some four hundred yards on their left, but John could clearly make out the figure of their Company Commander striding away ahead of his lads.

They didn't walk like this for very long, but pretty soon started to double from one place of cover to the next. It was quite different from the old days in the Desert when there was nothing else to be done but to walk straight ahead. There had been no vestage of cover in those days, but here, it was another kettle of fish. There were trees and little hillocks scattered all over the place. There were ditches in which a man might lie completely hidden from view, and a good many little white houses behind which it was possible to lie concealed while trying to spot where the enemy fire was coming from.

This was far more like European warfare than they had met during the whole course of the campaign in the Western Desert, and they liked the change. With all this cover to hide their advance, there was a decent chance of getting away with it. The question was how far it would last before they had to come out into the open to attack the fort.

John had clean forgotten the little force which was creeping round by the sea. He was all attention to the job in hand. He was like that : nothing ever mattered but the thing he happened to be doing at the moment, perhaps this was why he had been so successful as a soldier.

The Company had reached the edge of the cultivated part of the district, and were about to come out into the open at the foot of the steep slopes leading towards the fort. John had halted his little party in a deep ditch near the main road, and was watching through his glasses a point on the side of the hill from which machine-gun fire was evidently coming. The platoon on the right were held up, and couldn't get on because of this machine-gun post which had their position pretty well registered.

"Sergeant Major," said John, "send a runner back with this message to battalion." He took out a note book and scribbled a short message giving the map reference of the maching-gun post, as far as he could judge its position, and asked the C.O. to get the Gunners to have a go at knocking it out. It ought not to take long, he thought, to get a few rounds on to the place. Perhaps ten minutes after the runner's arrival at Battalion. There was bound to be an F.O.O.* of the Gunners there, and he would be in touch with his Regiment by wireless. Anyhow, it would be suicidal to try an advance without artillery support. The Gunners were firing all right, but none of their shells dropped anywhere near this particular place.

The runner departed on his mission, and John watched him flitting from hollow to hollow, taking advantage of every little piece of natural cover. Suddenly, the man lurched forward and fell on his face. There was no question as to what had happened. He had been hit by a stray bullet, and neatly knocked out as he ran.

"Runner down, Sir," cried the Sergeant Major, "shall I send another?"

---

* Forward Observation Officer.

"Yes please, and at once. Get him to grab the message from the other poor fellow out there, there isn't time to write another now, and every moment counts."

Another man was detailed to get back to the fallen runner, and he left the ditch at a fast trot. When he got to the man who had been hit, he bent down and seemed to be searching his body for the message. After a few moments he stood up, looked back and held the piece of paper up in his hand for the Company Commander to see that he had found it. With his free hand he made a gesture to convey that the man on the ground was dead, then he turned and disappeared running fast in the direction of Battalion Headquarters.

Within ten minutes the man was back to report to John that he had delivered the message to the Adjutant and that the Gunners had been asked to do what John had requested. There was nothing more to do now but wait for the shells to come down on the enemy. Sure enough, in about five more minutes, he heard them whistling over his head, and, looking through his glasses, saw them bursting all round the machine-gun post. The Platoon which had been pinned to the ground got to their feet and continued their advance without as much as a man being hit for several hundred yards. Then a couple of shells accounted for three of them, but from the machine-gun post, there was no fire. The Gunners had delivered the goods once again.

It was a bloody fight to gain that fort, and the Inverness Regiment lost many a good man on the forbidding slopes of that hill outside Homs. Gradually they worked their way up and it wasn't long before they got within close enough range for bayonet work. The defenders put up a stubborn resistance, but they had eventually to give way before the determined assault of the Highlanders. It was about five in the afternoon when the top of the hill was gained and the enemy chased out of the fort. A mixture of about hundred Germans and Italians were taken prisoner, but only after the fiercest hand-to-hand fighting.— When night came down on the battle-field, it found the Inverness Regiment in sole occupation of the feature they had been pleased to name 'Edinburgh Castle'.

* * *

Early next morning, the Signals Colonel was driving up the road in his Jeep. The Divisional Headquarters were on the move, and a great force of tanks waited behind for their chance to get across the intervening hills and down to the plains of Tripoli. The road twisted and wound among the mountains, very much like the Borderland between England and Scotland. Far away to the West, stretching for mile upon mile, were rolling hills which looked just as if they were covered with heather. It was, in fact, a tough kind of grass which grew thickly in the rocky ground, but looked like heather when seen from a distance, and the Colonel felt quite at home.

The battle had become very fluid, and the enemy had gone back quickly, only stopping here and there to let off some shells to delay the advance as long as possible. They had blown up every possible bridge and culvert, and the Engineers were hard at work repairing the damage so that the tanks and vehicles of the advancing army might pass through and get on down the road to distant Tripoli.

At the top of the pass, the Colonel stopped his Jeep and, getting out, clambered up the steep slopes of a small hill to see what sort of a view there was to be had from the top. When he got there, he was taken aback with the beauty of the scene which unfolded itself before him. Away to the North, almost at his feet, was the blue water of the Mediterranean, sparkling in the morning sun like diamonds. The great rollers were breaking on the beach, leaving behind a long line of white foam. Away to the right, back towards Homs, there were little clusters of palm trees marking the small villages scattered at random along the coast. The houses came to an end some four miles from Homs, and the coastline became broken where the hills ran right down to the water's edge. The shore was only two miles or so from the hill where the Colonel stood, but there were a couple of deep ravines between the road and the sea.

Away to the West, he could make out the winding ribbon of road stretching off to the distant horizon where patches of smoke marked explosions and burning vehicles. A few shells were still falling a couple of miles further on, but for the most part the place was pretty quiet. Down the road came an endless stream of vehicles, almost head to tail, and the Colonel wondered what would happen if the Luftwaffe decided to pay them a visit. But for days now there had been no sign of any enemy planes in the air. The R.A.F. had gained complete air superiority : a pleasant change after those terrible days during the retreat in France. The Highland Division were beginning to get a little bit of their own back.

In the middle distance, the hills grew less and less, and finally petered out into the rolling plain before Tripoli. The city itself was about sixty miles off, and not yet visible. In the green plain were many farm houses, like small white blobs. The place must have been very attractive in times of peace. Now, an army was advancing across this range of hills, and down into the broad plain below where the tanks would be able to manoeuvre and filter into the German lines. It was not clear where the enemy had got to. Some reports stated that Tripoli had fallen to the New Zealanders that morning and others affirmed that there were still small parties of the enemy between the hills and the city. It was a case of the Fog of War, and nobody really knew what was happening up in front.

Some more shells came down into the valley a little way ahead of where the Colonel was standing. Evidently the enemy was trying to register on the main road, and near the medium artillery batteries which had taken up positions on the left hand side a mile further on.

The Colonel clambered down to the road again and got back into his Jeep. They drove slowly on, threading their way between the hundreds of vehicles of all sorts and descriptions which filled the roadway. Luck held, and not one shell exploded anywhere within fifty yards of the highway. Just as well, for a fire would have spread rapidly with the vehicles almost touching each other for miles and miles on end.

When they got to Headquarters, they found that it was just a little valley in the hills, a short way off the road. There was no room for dispersion, but it wasn't necessary at this stage of the proceedings. There was no enemy aircraft in the air at all, and they would be moving on as soon as the road deviations were completed. A Conference was held later in the afternoon, which decided that nothing could be done to move the small Headquarters any further forward till the tanks had passed through.

There was a Brigade Headquarters a few hundred yards down the road, and the Colonel went there to see how they were getting on.

"Hullo Brian," he said as he came across the Signal Officer watching the traffic slowly winding down the hill to the first obstruction about half a mile away from where they stood.

"Hullo, Sir," replied the other, smiling a greeting to his superior. He was a tall, very good-looking officer of about thirty five years, and looked exceedingly bronzed and fit.

"What's your news, Brian?" asked the Colonel, filling his pipe from a much worn pouch.

"We're here for at least another couple of hours, Sir. We can't get on while all this stuff is blocking the road, and there are about three hundred tanks to pass along yet before we can get started."

"How long have you been here?"

"About six hours. There was a nasty little battle in these hills, and the Inverness Regiment lost about a hundred of their chaps. The Adjutant got taken prisoner, I'm afraid, but it was a good show, and they chased the Bosche out of it pretty quick. I came under machine-gun fire myself at one time. It was most disconcerting."

"I'll bet it was. Were any of those shells anywhere near here a few minutes ago?"

"Oh yes, they were," laughed Brian. "I was at the back of that hill, just where you are now, and I can tell you I spent quite a lot of time on my face. But the funny thing was the number of duds they sent over. There were about twenty five shells all told, and fully eithteen of them didn't explode. It was darned funny. You lay there listening to the screaming of the beastly things in the air as they came swishing over on top of us. Then, just as you expected them to explode, there would be a dull 'plop', and nothing more. It was a most eerie experience."

"But a darned useful one," grinned the Colonel. "I don't like hearing those horrible two owe five millimetre shells coming across. They sound exactly like an express train, and you feel as if you were lying in the middle of the rails waiting for the thing to run over you."

"How have the others got on, Sir? Have you any news?"

"Bobby's lot have done awfully well, Brian. In fact, everything has gone frightfully well. The wireless has worked like a dream, and I really think that the gilded Staff are beginning to appreciate our efforts. I once said that the only thanks Signals ever get for a job well done is a slight, a very slight, diminution of abuse. But it's not quite true."

Brian laughed. "There's a lot of truth in it anyway, Sir," he chuckled. "My lads have done awfully well too, but I'll be glad when we get to Tripoli, and they can get down to it and sleep the clock round."

"I'm a bit sleepy myself, Brian," remarked the Colonel. He hadn't had his clothes off since the night before the battle of the Wadi Chebir, and he felt horribly dirty and grimy. But he was in good heart and felt that he could carry on almost indefinitely now.

They walked down to have a look at the deviation which the Sappers had constructed. The road ran down the side of a small ravine, and the track had been cut out of the hillside. A whole portion of the road had been blown clean out, and the Sappers had worked like niggers to fill in a temporary surface, to allow the hundreds of waiting vehicles and tanks to pass across the gap. It had been completed a couple of hours earlier, but only one vehicle at a time could tackle the dangerous crossing, so it was a slow business.

As it got nearly dark, they decided to filter the various vehicles of the Divisional Battle Headquarters out on the road, and get them on into Tripoli as quickly as they could. The Colonel went off in his Jeep with only just enough petrol to complete the journey. It was getting very short indeed, and many drivers were begging cans off their more lucky brethren.

It was a horrible run, especially after dark. There was no moon, and literally hundreds of vehicles on the road, nose to tail all the way. There were about seven deviations where the Germans had blown the bridges, and Sappers, assisted by toiling infantry were labouring like slaves to get them completed. The tanks had simply got to get through and continue chasing the fleeing Hun, and every man who could be brought to the scene of a demolition was rushed forward.

It was a wonderful tribute to the discipline and spirit of comradship of the Highland Division that these deviations were constructed so quickly. The Colonel came across many little groups of private soldiers, without officers or N.C.O's, making their weary way from one scene of operations to the next, and in some cases this meant a walk of five or six miles at a stretch. Without leaders, these little bands of men might easily have given up and sat down by the roadside to rest and wait for some lorry to give them a lift. They had all fought a long battle and for forty eight hours had little water and less food. And yet they kept at it, and dug like beavers wherever they were required. Some of them were dead beat, but they never gave in till the last deviation had been completed. Such was the indomitable spirit of the Highland Division. The great tradition of the Division gained in the last War had been worthily upheld.

All through the night the work went on, and the tanks and lorries came streaming along the plain in the direction of the Capital of Tripolitania. It was about five in the morning when the first armoured cars entered the city. They found it a place of the dead. Not a soul was to be seen in all the deserted streets.

The Highlanders arrived just after it began to get light. They at once made for the key places, like the harbour and the docks. There were no Germans to be found, for they had departed from the scene several hours before. The rising sun found the Union Jack floating bravely in the morning breeze above the entrance to the harbour.

The King of Italy had lost the last of his foreign possessions. The Italian nation no longer had an Empire. From the city square of Tripoli came the sound of the bagpipes. The Pipe Major of a famous battalion was playing the Regimental Tunes of the Five Highland Regiments.

CHAPTER XVI

EPILOGUE

It was a Sunday morning in November 1942, and a cold East wind was blowing in from the sea, searching out the nooks and crannies of the city of Edinburgh. A thin powdering of snow lay on the Meadows, but no more was falling now, although the sky was still overcast with big grey clouds.

John Crighton W.S. looked out of the dining-room window of his flat in Warrender Park Crescent, and decided that it was far too unpleasant a day to go out. He had had a long and anxious week at the office and he needed a day of relaxation. He was a man holding a good position, and had made a name for himself in his profession; in fact, by now he was the senior partner in his firm.

It was a particularly cold and bleak Sunday morning, and James Crighton decided to stay in by the fireside and read the papers rather than essay outside to catch his death of cold in search of exercise.

He was alone in the room, his wife being busy about the house. Their one servant was away for the week-end and Mrs. Crighton was holding the fort until the girl returned. James Crighton turned away from the window and walked back to the warmth of the hearth where a goodly log fire was burning. He took down a pipe from the mantle-piece and started to fill it.

As he did so, his eyes travelled up from the fire to a picture which hung above the mantle-piece. It was the photograph of a young officer, dressed in the uniform of a famous Highland Regiment. He was a cheery looking youngster with dark, wavy hair brushed back from a high, intelligent forehead. He had the fresh, healthy look of the rugger player; and well he might, for 'Jock' Crighton had appeared on three successive occasions for the Scottish Fifteen before the war had come to end all these things.

The Crightons knew that their only son was now serving with his Regiment somewhere in the Middle East, for he had been home on embarkation leave last summer. Whether he was now involved in the fighting in the Western Desert, they could only guess. The Wireless News had reported the presence of Scottish Units in the Desert, and they naturally concluded that their Jock must be there in the thick of it.

John Crighton was almighty proud of his boy; and well he might be, for not only was the lad a rugger International of some repute, but he had been doing exceptionally well at the University until he had gone off with the Territorial battalion he was now in.

The man picked up a paper and subsided into a deep arm chair at the side of the fire-place. For about an hour he read steadily, and then he laid down the paper and gave himself up to his thoughts. How well he remembered that eventful night about two weeks ago when he and his wife had been sitting up listening to the Wireless. It had been about eleven o'clock at night and there was a dance programme on.

The two of them had sat and listened to the dance music for about half an hour, and were just about to retire to bed, when the programme had been suddenly interrupted. The Announcer's voice had broken into the programme, and listeners were told to "Stand by for an important announcement from Cairo". What had happened? We had only lately lost Tobruk, and things had not been going any too well in the Middle East. Was this to tell of the loss of the whole of the Middle East? Had we lost our hold on Egypt? Then had come the tremendous news.

"From Middle East Headquarters Cairo comes the announcement that the Middle East forces attacked on the night of October 23rd. The Axis forces in the Western Desert, after twelve days and nights of ceaseless attacks by our land and air forces, are now in full retreat."

"Their disordered columns are being relentlessly attacked by our land forces, and by the allied air force by day and night."

"It is known that the enemy's losses in killed and wounded have been exceptionally high."

John Crighton smiled to himself as he remembered how he and his wife had drunk a small nightcap in honour of the great victory, and to the safe return of their boy. He remained deep in thought, and after a little while his wife came in and sat down for a while before starting to prepare their lunch. It was close on twelve o'clock, and neither of them spoke for several minutes.

Suddenly Jean Crighton pricked up her ears.

"What's that noise, John? Do you hear it?"

"What noise, Jean? I don't hear anything unusual."

Then he remembered, and stood up, listening. After a few moments he walked over to the window and threw up the bottom sash. From outside, filling the crisp morning air with tumultuous music, sounding across the open spaces of the Meadows and seeking out every nook and cranny of the ancient Scottish Capital, came resounding the one sound which had been absent ever since the war began.

John Crighton came back to the fireplace and gave his wife a huge hug. Together they looked up at the picture of their boy.

The Church Bells were ringing out to commemorate the great victory at El Alamein.